Published in the United States of America
By Family Solutions Publishing, LLC
All Rights Reserved
Do not duplicate without written permission.

All scripture references are King James Version unless
otherwise indicated.

Book Design by: FSI Publishing, LLC.

Printed in the United States of America by
Family Solutions Publishing, LLC.
1716 West State Highway 152
Mustang, OK 73064

Publisher's Cataloging in Publication

Harris, Connie and Sidebottom, Sharolyn

No Time For Goodbyes/Connie Harris and Sharolyn Sidebottom

Originally published: Mustang, OK: Family Solutions Pub.:2003

1. Spiritual Life - protestant 2. Self-Help 3. Family

ISBN 0-9740939-4-7 $12.95

Dedication

This writing is dedicated in loving memory of our husbands, Lee Harris and Jerry Sidebottom. By their living they taught us to live lives of integrity and honor and exemplified the love of the Father to us. They remained steady, constant, covenant-hearted men even in the midst of all the ups and downs of marriage and family living. In dying, they taught us to understand the sovereignty of God and His grace.

We would like to thank Connie's children, David and Sandy Harris, Kellie and Nick Moore, Stacy and Jason Brown, and Sharolyn's children, Nathan, Brian, and Jonathan Sidebottom for their loving support and allowing us to share our story.

We would also like to express our appreciation to all of our family, friends, and church family who helped us with so many different things, supported us, and prayed for us through all we have experienced. So many were there for us when we needed them that they are too numerous to mention, but we have all your kindness tucked in our hearts as priceless treasures of the relationship we share.

Table of Contents

Foreword

Dredging up memories has been an emotional challenge for us. We have written and wept as we have poured our hearts out in the pages of this book. The only reason we have relived these memories, writing them down, is in the hopes that God will make what we have found through our sorrow nourishment to those who read. We pray you will be encouraged in your walk of faith to go to the next level in the depth of His love.

It is not what happens to us that matters. It is what happens *in* us because of what happens *to* us that makes the difference. If you are in the midst of crushing difficulties, "Don't quit!" If more than one thing is happening to you at a time, "Take heart!" You are growing! The joy of knowing God more intimately is set before you.

The experiences we shared together have been distressing. The multiplicity of events, have "dinged" our lives, but we have discovered the "dings" to be opportunities to declare the goodness and mercy of God as we have looked beyond the event to His glory. His grace has been so sufficient as we have leaned into Him. Things began happening so fast to us that we were insufficient in our own strength to handle the emotions, let alone the circumstances. But God, in His grace and mercy enveloped us in His love, and we found nothing could separate us from His love.

In our journey we have discovered life itself is by His mercy. We have been humbled and at the same time filled with confidence and boldness, as we have never experienced before. Not in ourselves, but in the wonderful love of our Father.

It is much like the antique cabinet that shows many "dings" of usage throughout nearly two centuries of service to a family. Every "ding" has a story of its own, but even with all the "dings" it continues to serve the purpose it was created to do. The "dings" add character to the piece, even increasing its value to those who treasure it. Its quality and craftsmanship has stood the test of time.

Regardless of our function in this life, we were created to be reflections of His image. Life will "ding" you. The "dings" of life can either be viewed as damaged places or added character, increasing our value to the Father. We are to be witnesses to the glory and character of God and only if we have to, use words. People are watching our lives even when we don't realize it, and our actions speak so much louder than our words.

Many times throughout the last 18 months people have told Connie and me what "strong women" we are. If there is any strength in our lives it is because we have surrendered to the grace of our Father God and His strength is made perfect in our weakness. Only through our surrender to the Father can any of us be of any value to Him as we stand the test of the "dings" of time bringing glory and honor to His name.

Introduction

Sometimes there are unexpected twists and turns on the road of life. David, in Psalm 23, painted a very clear word picture of what the path of life can look like. Sometimes the Lord who is our Shepherd causes us to lie down in fresh green pastures and leads us beside still and restful waters. In those times He refreshes and restores our soul on the pathway of our life. He also "leads us in paths that will bring us into His righteousness causing us to walk in uprightness and right standing with Him.

It is not by our righteousness we come into right standing with Him. We can't earn righteousness. We must learn to surrender to it. Yes, sometimes the path to His righteousness leads us through the deep, sunless valley of the shadow of death. In this valley, He teaches us to fear or dread no evil. In the darkness, we discover He is still with us, and He will never leave us or forsake us. His rod protects us by correcting us or fighting for us. His staff guides us, supports us, and sustains us. His rod and staff together are comfort to us.

He continues to feed me at His table in the midst of my trouble, affliction, or distress. He anoints my head, that part of me that is so easily shaken when trouble comes, with oil, the richness of His Holy Spirit so that my thoughts will be staid on Him. He fills the cup of my life, full to the brim, running over with Himself. Surely goodness, mercy, and unfailing love shall follow me all the days of my life. Throughout the length of my days, the house of the Lord and His presence shall be my dwelling place.

Our faith has to be rooted, and grounded in His grace, mercy, and unfailing love. Nothing can separate us from the love of God. Our faith cannot be based upon our experiences or circumstances, whether they are good or bad. We have equated faith with all of life's circumstances being good. Faith, however, is our personal surrender to the Father, and drinking the cup of our experiences whether they are good or bad in communion with Him.

Experiences alone are not an end in themselves. Experiences are a gateway to knowing the love, mercy, and grace of God for ourselves, which far surpasses just mere knowledge without experience. Through practical experience with the love of God in good times and bad, He fills us with His divine presence. It is out of that indwelling presence He "is able to carry out His purpose and do super-abundantly, far over and above all that we ask or think infinitely beyond our highest prayers, desires, thoughts, hopes, or dreams." Ephesians 3:20

We know we cannot give you what we have, but we hope

within the content of these pages we make you homesick for the Presence, Peace, and Love of our Lord Jesus Christ we have found. Your sisters in Christ—Sharolyn and Connie

Chapter One

Family Ties

~Sharolyn~

An interoffice memo from Jerry's employment caught my attention: Cruise to the Bahamas for $79.00 per person aboard the Discovery. How exciting! I met Lee in the Sunday school hallway of our church the very next Sunday morning with ad in hand. "Lee! What would you think of surprising our mates with a trip to the Bahamas for their birthdays?" Both Jerry and Connie's birthdays were in the month of May. Lee jumped at the chance, and we began planning the surprise.

Lee asked Connie sometime later if I had said anything to her. He just couldn't keep the secret any longer and had to tell her what we were planning. Of course, when Connie discovered the surprise, she began playing with my mind just to see if she could make me talk but I never did. Finally, the four of us were out to eat one night when Connie couldn't keep silent any longer.

The cat was out of the bag and everyone knew we were going to the Bahamas. The year was 1999, and what a wonderful trip we had!

We decided, instead of flying, we would take a road trip to Ft. Lauderdale, Florida. A total of six days on the road plus four days in Freeport, Bahamas made for a 10-day trip. The beaches were beautiful. We snorkeled, parasailed, and attended a beach barbeque. We toured an arboretum filled with beautiful foliage and exotic birds. Our men decided to feed the birds. As soon as they placed the quarters in the seed dispenser, birds began landing on their heads and shoulders. The shock on their faces was priceless and laughter filled the air.

~Connie~

As we were leaving Georgia on the way home, Lee began planning our next couple get-away. I was amazed with what God was doing with our families. God had so changed Lee's heart to encompass another family into our family nucleus. Lee had never wanted to vacation with anyone outside of the family. Being a manager of Wal-Mart he was with people all of the time and his family were the only ones with whom he wanted to spend quality time.

~Sharolyn~

There had never been a couple that Jerry and I could have

spent ten days with and truly enjoyed it enough to plan another trip. When we had time off, the last thing we wanted to do was spend it with people outside of our family. In pastoral care I was with people all the time visiting or counseling. A pastor's job seems to be 2nd shift so Jerry and our sons would see me very little in the evenings. When we could get away, he wanted it to be just us.

It really was amazing that the Bahamas trip got off the ground, but God was extending the borders of the covenant He had placed between Connie and I to include our families. Little did we know what lay ahead for our families as we danced in the moonlight to the music on the cruise ship as we returned to Florida!

An Unlikely Friendship

~Sharolyn~

Connie was a volunteer receptionist a couple of days a week at the church where I was on staff. Frankly, I hardly noticed her other than to say good morning. Life can be lonely at times in the ministry, and I was experiencing one of those lonely seasons. In July of 1998, she asked if we could go to lunch as she had something she wanted to discuss with me. I did a lot of counseling at the church, so we met for lunch to discuss her concern. It was a very generic lunch, and we returned to business as usual. After the lunch date, we seemed to visit more at the office.

~Connie~

In volunteering as a receptionist at The Father's House, I began to get to know the staff of the church. Sharolyn seemed to be a very focused, lonely person, with little time for enjoying life. With my personality (Sanguine) I like to tease and joke with people to get them to lighten up. I began joking with Sharolyn when she would pass by my desk. She would laugh a little, but she didn't seem to want a friendship. I continued to give her a hard time anyway.

~Sharolyn~

At the end of August of 1998, our church was hosting our annual women's seminar. It was a weekend event. Friday night, I was on stage as a part of the worship team and at the end of the service, I looked across the room and saw Connie. Suddenly, I knew God had a word of encouragement for her. Leaving my post on stage, I made my way across the auditorium. She saw me coming like a woman with a mission. When I delivered the message of exhortation and laid my hands on her, the power of God came and instantly filled my heart with love for her. My mind was saying, "My God, what is this? I barely even know this woman!" Connie was on the floor; the power of God was so strong. Looking up at me, she asked what I was sensing in the spirit. I was so shocked at the love God had instantly put in my heart for her. I didn't know what to say. I hugged her and muttered some kind of a blessing and went back to the stage. This was something I had to get my mind around.

~Connie~

Saturday morning we gathered back at the church for the second day of meetings. While I was worshipping, I looked over at Sharolyn on stage worshipping the Father and playing the keyboard. God suddenly gave me such a love for her. I couldn't imagine what was happening. I hardly knew her. I asked Sharolyn to have lunch with me after the service Saturday. Somehow we began communicating to the other person the love that God had placed in our hearts that weekend and our hearts were instantly joined together. This had to be God because I am such a private person. I allowed very few people, other than my husband, to get close to me.

~Sharolyn~

The entire first year of this new relationship, God allowed us to spend a great deal of time together. Our husbands accused us of being joined at the hip or Siamese twins. The strangest thing about our friendship was how completely opposite we were about everything. Connie shopped the malls, loved to just have fun, and could be the life of any party. I am a Choleric/Melancholy blend personality, shopped Home Depot, was very task oriented, and loved a good home improvement project that involved using a hammer and saw. Basically, I'm a work-a-holic, everything had to have a purpose, and time was always of the essence. Connie, on the other hand, was a "died in the wool" shopper, and time . . .? What is time when there is a 50% off, plus an additional 25% off, and a coupon for yet another 15%? "Why, they are paying me to take these clothes out of the store!" You guessed it! I'm a power shopper. Get it, bag it, and get out!

We discovered to have a relationship we would have to learn to be a part of the other's world. Connie began dragging me around to malls. I had no idea what an art it was to shop. There were rhythms to sales. Prices rose and fell according to days of the week and times of the year. Being taught the "mall" ropes by a veteran shopper was amazing. It was a novel idea to actually buy something without a need, and shop according to this national rhythm of seasonal clearances. I must admit in the early days I was bored out of my gourd and out of shopping steam before Connie had truly even begun to shop.

On the other hand, put me in a Home Depot or Lowe's and I could shop with energy to spare. Sales were nice but shopping was on a need basis. Either something was broken, and needed replaced, or fixed, or a brainy idea had popped into my head for a home improvement project that would make life easier. These were the kind of stores where Connie would run out of shopping energy. The thought raced through both of our minds as we were forced to shop in each other's store of expertise "Will she never quit?!" followed with prayers for supernatural intervention, "God deliver me!"

Then there were the actual projects. If people were to really spend time with me, they would have to become a part of my project. Connie had never held a hammer in her hand other than handing it off to someone else to use. Not so anymore! Jerry and I had purchased a country home that needed a lot of remodel and repair, and if Connie was going to spend time with me, she was going to learn to shingle a roof and side a house. How I remember the first time she hit the wrong nail! Not good!

Those in the church who knew both our stations in life were amazed that a utility company worker could have anything in common with Wal-Mart management. It's much like the story of David, the shepherd boy, having a relationship with Jonathan, the King's son. Economically we were worlds apart, yet God had put us together. When I first understood the extreme differences in our household incomes, I wanted to shy away from the relationship. How could we possibly contribute or keep up socially in such an economically lopsided friendship, but God doesn't seem to care about economics. He puts people together to bring about His will and purpose in their lives.

If God had not put us together the way He did, we would not have had a friendship, our lives were just too different. There were many times disagreements would surface. We would become so angry with the other person that nothing in us wanted to remain friends, but we knew God had put us together, so for the sake of the covenant we began to say, "Just walk with me. I don't like you right now. You've offended me, but I know God put us together so walk with me." We know now that saying, "walk with me" allowed God's grace the opportunity to enter the breach in our relationship and put us back together even stronger than we were before.

"Holy Ghost setups" began to occur as we were together. That's the term we gave the occasions in which past, or present events of failures, or hidden ugliness would surface for us to deal with. Sometimes these were wounds inflicted on us by others. God gave us a special grace to be transparent with the other person and an unconditional love to cover the other person regardless of the ugliness.

We all have these burial sites in the emotional soil of our lives that we don't want anyone but God to see. If anyone gets close to our burial ground, the emotional warrior (usually anger) commissioned to guard the site, rises up in defense against the perpetrator. Our burial sites become unproductive soil in our lives. They are untouchable "dead works" in need of the unconditional love of God through another person to cleanse and heal them from our lives.

God began to make very real to us the need to confess our faults to each other that we could be healed. We had both confessed our faults and sins to our Lord and Savior Jesus Christ. We had also been transparent with our husbands, but there was something about the love of God flowing through another person who didn't have to continue being our friend, that began to heal us. That caused those burial sites to produce life again.

God began to teach us unconditional love. That wasn't something we came by naturally. His grace enabled us to love each other regardless, in spite of, no matter what, forever, and for always. Believe us when we tell you the differences in our personalities gave us many opportunities to love the other person "in spite of." Now, in the light of the events that have happened in our lives, we are so grateful God put us together the way He did and taught us to walk together in covenant relationship. We had no idea that God was preparing us for the days that were ahead.

God not only put Connie and me together, but He put our husbands and our children together. Our children were still young when Lee and Connie committed to caring for them if something were to happen to Jerry and me prematurely. It takes a special relationship to commit to another family's children outside of your own biological family.

We certainly were not surprised that others were amazed at our friendship. We were amazed ourselves, but less than a year after Connie and I met, the four of us were vacationing.

Chapter Two

The River of Grief

~Connie~

It was Wednesday, Lee's day off, and I wasn't able to sleep late. I looked over at Lee snoozing away. I got up as quietly as I could to make coffee and start my day. Lee usually rose early even on his days off, but this particular morning he slept until around 9 AM. Then, I fixed his favorite breakfast and we watched TV a while. As we were sitting there, Lee said something that ticked me off, but I didn't say anything. I just started to deal with my emotions and acted like everything was okay. Lee decided to go play golf and get his haircut, and I was going to attend the ladies luncheon. After the luncheon, I had shopping on my mind.

I had purchased a diamond solitaire a few days earlier, and felt like God was telling me to take it back. Lee and I had talked it over and we didn't know if we wanted to spend that kind of money on a ring right then. When I got to the parking lot to return the ring, I felt like I wasn't supposed to take it back. "God which is it, keep it or take it back?" I called Sharolyn to meet me in the McDonalds parking lot to talk over my dilemma. Looking back, we realize God was directing our steps so Sharolyn would be with me when I got the call.

After playing golf, Lee had gone to get a haircut. The barber greeted him, and asked him how he was doing. Lee said he wasn't doing so well. The barber said he wasn't feeling well either. Lee sat down in the chair while the barber continued to talk. Suddenly, the barber looked at Lee and asked him if he was feeling all right. Lee said he wasn't and that his chest was hurting. The barber suspected he was having a heart attack and called 911 and Wal-Mart. He didn't know how to contact me directly. He went next door to see if someone knew CPR, and they began working on Lee before the ambulance got there.

Around 1:30 that afternoon, while Sharolyn and I were sitting at McDonalds, I received a call from Lee's assistant manager. I was told Lee was having trouble breathing, and was being taken to Hutchinson hospital via ambulance. In my mind Lee was in perfect health, and there was no way that he could be having physical problems. He was really all right. I just knew it; however, my body must have known otherwise. Sharolyn started patting my knee trying to console me, but it physically hurt for her to touch me. I told her to stop touching me. We rushed to the hospital.

While waiting for the ambulance to arrive, I just kept saying I knew it wasn't his heart. He just had a physical in December of 2000, and the doctor said he would live to be 90. I really thought it was just a heat stroke. Lee was always in such good health.

Finally, the ambulance arrived and they announced it as a code blue. I had no idea what a code blue was. They brought him in and continued working on him. They finally let me in to see him. His eyes were rolled back in his head, and his chest was blue from them trying to restart his heart. I just couldn't believe this was happening. I prayed and cried out to God not to take his arms away from me. I had to leave the room. Our pastor was trying to console me, and told me to keep believing in God. All I could think was, *Please God, don't take his arms from me*. They continued working on him for quite awhile. I went back into the room begging Lee to come back to me. The hospital staff continued to work, and I had to leave the room again. I tried to care for the girls and comfort them, but I felt so scattered I didn't really know what to do. Finally, they came out and told me, "Mrs. Harris there is nothing else we can do. We're sorry your husband didn't make it."

I felt like it was all just a bad dream and I would wake up soon. I couldn't believe this was really happening. I called David, our oldest child, and told him his daddy had died. He started screaming over the phone, "This can't happen to my daddy." The girls were weeping beside me in disbelief that this could be happening to their daddy. He was one of the healthiest, most active men they knew.

Sharolyn drove us home from the hospital. Our church, family, and friends were so supportive, helping us with all of the many details. Some of the women of our church came to our home to make sure we were ready for company. I began to think of all of the people who needed to be called, and began calling my family.

Eventually, I found myself downstairs alone, my mind racing with thoughts of how upset I had been with Lee over what he had said that morning. This wasn't the first time I had become upset with my husband over something he had said, but it was the first time I was not able to talk it through with him. After we parted Wednesday morning, I never spoke to him again.

Sometimes we don't have days to deal with offences. If we need to forgive someone, or ask them to forgive us, or get out in the open what is troubling us, we need to do it immediately so the enemy can't beat us up later. Lee had no idea I was upset with him that morning. To this day, the enemy stills tries to bring it back to my mind to cause regret, but the Father continues to tell me to give it to Him. I am forgiven!

Funeral arrangements had to be made, and difficult

questions had to be answered. When do you want to have the service? Where do you want to have the service? Oh! Where *should* we have the service? Kellie will be married in our church in seven weeks! We can't have the memory of daddy's coffin at the front of the church during what should be a joyous occasion! Who will be officiating? What songs do we want? What do you want Lee to wear? Which coffin do you want? Where will he be buried? And finally, what will be your method of payment?

Our church served a meal for the family the day of the funeral. Everything seemed to be going fine when it hit me what we were there for. Lee was gone and I started to cry. I tried to walk away from the table as casually as I could so no one would follow me, but my son David saw me leave and followed. I went into the women's bathroom crying and David, never a shy man, followed me in. He began to hold me in his arms and I began to pray in the Holy Spirit. David began to say, "I am your strength and your rock, lean into me. I will never leave you nor forsake you." I started praising God when David began to speak. David had been away from the Lord for several years but this moment gave me hope that God was bringing David back to Himself. Sharolyn was with us and told me that God had given her the same word, but the Holy Spirit told her to keep silent. God is so good and He loves us so much.

When we arrived at the church for the funeral, they ushered the family into a room off to the side until all the people were seated. Everything had happened so fast; I was in a daze. What were we doing here? The service began with different speakers, and then we started to sing the song "Fragrant Offering." That was one of Lee's favorite songs and I started to weep. I stood to my feet and started to worship the Father, and my family stood with me. The Father's grace was so amazing. In the midst of so much pain, out of our spirits came so much worship to the Father.

~Sharolyn~

There were over 750 people in attendance at Lee's funeral. Helping with Lee's service was one of the hardest things I have ever had to do. Prior to the service, I closed the door to my office and cried out to God, "I worship, I worship. I don't understand, but You are sovereign."

The strength that God was giving Connie was amazing. She stood and greeted everyone that had come to the funeral with a hug or a handshake. The night before the funeral, the Wal-Mart associates had a memorial service in the parking lot after the store closed at 11 P.M. where another 200 – 300 people attended and she greeted all of them. As people were coming through to greet Connie and view Lee's body, one of our friends whispered to me, "This has struck too close to home." I agreed with her. Little did I know how close to home it really was!

So many questions and so many emotions were swirling and the next few days were a blur. The prevailing question in our minds was, "If God holds the number of our days in his hand, what would a few more days have mattered?" Why could Lee not have given his oldest daughter away on her wedding day in just seven weeks? There were still so many plans and details to take care of for the wedding. Connie needed him. He was so level headed, stable, and logical. All this seemed so horrible.

The emotions were overwhelming. Unless you have walked here, you have no clue as to the many different emotions that you can have all at once. It felt like anger, pain, grief, fear, and frustration were battling for center stage all at the same time. Physically, everyone was going through the motions, but inside there was such pain and brokenness it was amazing that the body continued to move forward. My husband Jerry and I have both lost siblings, but those losses fade in comparison to the grief we felt losing our best friend whom we had shared so much life with. From time to time there was a lull in the grief. Maybe a memory produced some laughter or a visitor started a conversation that took our mind off the pain for a moment but then the mind would wander again to the reason we were together and grief pressed in.

It is hard to know what to say at a time like this, particularly when it is an off-time death (unexpected or premature death). We can tell you from experience what words brought comfort and what grated on our nerves. Lee's death so broadsided Connie and the children, and Jerry and I, and the boys, that when any of us were asked how we were doing our gut response was "How do you think we're doing?!" Connie has just lost her soul mate and the love of her life. The children have lost their father and best friend with no warning. Jerry and I have lost our best friend who had become more than a brother to us and our boys have lost their second dad. Do you really want to know how we are doing? But the answer we would say was "okay." Lee's death was such a tremendous shock and jolt to everyone's emotions.

"Sorry about your loss," clanged in our ears. "If I hear the word 'loss' one more time I'll scream." We didn't need to be reminded of our "loss." "I love you and I am praying for you" seemed to give the most comfort because it required only a "thank you" response and that is what everyone needed—love and prayer.

When Connie would be asked what could be done for her, she didn't know. Her mind was on a one-way track. Her emotions began to scream, "Questions! Please, no more questions! Don't make me have to find a response that I have to think about." Household chores seemed so trivial to her. Things just didn't matter. Everything about her was on tilt. She didn't have a clue what she needed or didn't need. All she knew was *who* she needed was gone and all else paled in comparison. If something did come to mind, she would blurt it out to whomever was there to listen.

What used to be a simple task of picking up a few items

at the store now had turned into a one-way thought pattern. She would go for three or four items and maybe come back with one item. That would cause more frustration. "Why can't I remember what I need to get?"

"Oh Father, what is this road we are walking? Will we ever be able to look back at this and understand?" Lee, of all people! He had such a servant's heart. People came from everywhere saying if it weren't for Lee we would have lost our house, or our job. One woman said he raised money for her to have a liver transplant. Someone bought rock from the store with no way to haul it so Lee delivered it in his own truck. An older person bought a tree and was unable to plant it, so Lee made a house call and planted the tree. No one will ever know but God all that Lee did for others. Connie didn't even know! No wonder the church was full. He had touched so many lives because he genuinely loved and cared for people.

Our families have walked in such a covenant of love that the grief seems to be that of one family. My sons were sobbing at the loss of their second dad. Lee had hired Nathan to work for him at Wal-Mart. He had taken Nathan under his wing and Nathan didn't think there was anything Lee couldn't do. Lee attended Brian's football games. Lee and Jerry could become extremely undignified in the stands. Jonathan thought he was the "coolest." I have never heard my husband cry with such anguish. Jerry and

I would hold each other through the night, but in our embrace my heart cried out for my sister whose arms were empty and who would never feel Lee's arms around her again and more tears gushed.

The difficulty is in knowing what to do when emotions are so messed up and the playing field is so totally different when an off-time death occurs. I wanted to protect Connie and the kids from pain and grief, but I couldn't. Grief is very real and must be embraced and walked through. Every member of the family has to walk through it in their own way. Many times in the last few days what I wanted to do and give wasn't what was needed or wanted at all. I have felt my need to wrap Connie up in my arms and comfort her, but her emotions are saying, "Don't touch me!" When people would touch her or hug her, she would literally feel physical pain. She seemed to hold everyone at arm's length.

A premise for many breakups in relationships is becoming offended or taking it personally when the way we want to love the other person is rejected. It is hard to walk with people where they are, especially when we have never walked where they are walking. Even if we have walked there, no two people will react the same way. Connie is the one leading this walk right now. I have to be sensitive to follow her lead and walk with her according to her needs and not my own.

Connie is going through the darkest days of her life. I

know there will be lots of rough places we will have to walk through ahead. The path is unknown. I can't tell her how to handle these rough places, but I can lend my strength to support her along the path. When we finish this path, our lives, our perspectives, our purposes will all be altered in some way, but we will walk together and we will make it through. God's grace is sufficient. That is covenant!

Right now emotions are raw for both of our families; exposed for all to see. This is as transparent as it gets. Sometimes her response to my "help" hurts. There were times I felt I had lost both Lee and Connie. She was numb, but still going through the motions while hurting beyond belief. Emotionally she was unable to give or receive. Hugs were given, words were said, but nothing seemed to penetrate below the surface of the skin. I felt alienated from the best friend I knew and loved, so my response was to fly into a flurry of activity. There was laundry to be done and food to be set out for the multitude of family that descended upon her home. She needed someone to host the flood of company with maid service and, I gladly did just that.

God will use many people to speak healing into her life. She needs stories to make her laugh. The words that use to flow so easily out of my spirit that would cause laughter in her are not there. All I felt was her grief and her pain and there was no initiative of laughter in me. When a story was told, it seemed everyone experienced laughter on the outside while continuing to weep on the inside. Emotions were extreme. Laughter was hysterical, while weeping gushed from the core our beings, but somehow both seemed to remove the grief by increments.

~Connie~

The next day after the funeral in Hutchinson, we began our trip to Witt Springs, Arkansas to bury Lee. We buried him in a little country cemetery where other family members are buried. We were traveling on our daughter, Stacy's, 21st birthday. We stopped in Springfield, Missouri for her birthday dinner. We tried to make the day as normal as possible for her. It is our family custom to take the birthday person out to eat at the restaurant of their choice. As we sat down, Lee was missing from the table. What a void was left in our lives. Stacy's father had never missed any of his children's birthday celebrations. How do we go on now without him? David is quite a card when he wants to be and by God's grace he had us all laughing through the birthday dinner. We traveled on to Harrison, Arkansas and stopped for the night before the graveside service the next day.

~Sharolyn~

The day we buried Lee's body, I was awakened at 4:00A.M. and began to pray for my friend. The words that prayed out of me amazed me. I prayed that the anointing on Lee's life would be revealed in every member of the family and that a double portion of the strength, wisdom, steadfastness, patience, ability, logic, caring, giving, discernment, ability to gain wealth, and all other good he possessed would be in and rest upon each member of his household even as Elijah's mantle was passed on to Elisha with a double portion. It did not seem right for Lee's mantle to leave with him, but that it should pass to his family.

My husband was awakened by my prayers and began praying in agreement with what the Spirit was praying through me. When the spirit of prayer left us at 5:15 A.M., we went back to sleep for 45 minutes and I slept with a peace I had not experienced since the day of Lee's death. Such a calm assurance came over me; I knew everything would be all right.

~Connie~

When we arrived at Witt Springs, we were served a lunch at the country church and a whole new group of people began to share their condolences. We made the short trip from the church to the little country cemetery where Lee's family and Arkansas friends had gathered. Lee's brothers and sister were so broken because we were laying their little brother in the ground. In a few short minutes final goodbyes to the body that housed my husband, Lee Harris, had been said.

Our pastor brought golf balls and a club to the graveside service. After the service, our children honored their dad by hitting some golf balls into the woods. Lee truly enjoyed playing golf. I stood at the side of his casket to say final goodbyes to my husband of 27 years. These were supposed to be the best years of our lives. Lee was going to retire within a couple of years and our plans were to travel. Now, everything was changed.

-Sharolyn-

Then, in the old country cemetery, they lowered the vault and cleared off the tent. Connie's brothers began shoveling the dirt in the hole until the grave was covered. Jerry and I had never experienced that kind of closure before. Somehow watching those men fill in the grave of the man they had loved for so many years brought warmth and love I had never experienced in the cold professional settings of my Kansas Cemeteries. I could see tension being released from my dear friend as she relaxed, and a glimmer of the Connie I knew before Lee's death began to come back.

~Connie~

We returned to Wichita in time to take David and his wife Sandy to the airport. It was so hard to see my son board the plane. I had lost Lee and I just wanted to gather my children all around me. Now, the girls and I were alone and we drove home silently lost in our own grief. When we arrived home it was Wednesday night and we couldn't decide whether we wanted to go to church that night or not. We finally decided to go to Down Town Church, which is our youth church.

We started worshipping and there was a young girl sobbing

on the last row who caught my attention. I went to pray for her, and while I was standing behind her the Holy Spirit began to speak to me. He told me that it wasn't about me. It wasn't about my pain, but it was about Him and His glory. If I would give out of my pain He would fill me up with Himself. There came such a joy in me and my pain was gone. If we don't give out even in the midst of pain, then we are still full of ourselves and there is no room for Him to put anything in us.

I wish I could say that my pain never came back, but it did. When I focused on myself and what I'd lost, it would take me into deep grief. God taught me in those times to speak out of my heart, "I worship," and His grace would come in and remove the pain and bring peace to my heart. I couldn't understand how just saying "I worship" could speak peace to my pain. The Holy Spirit taught me that my willingness to speak "I worship," even though it didn't feel or look like I was worshipping, allowed His grace to change my emotions.

I began to see how at Lee's funeral in the midst of our deepest pain, God had helped us to glorify Him. There were people at Lee's funeral that were not born again and possibly would never have heard the gospel any other way. Some have given their hearts to the Lord since that day. There are others that attended who, as yet, have not accepted the Lord that I am continuing to minister to as God puts them in my pathway.

~Sharolyn~

On the way home from Arkansas I finished writing in my journal the contents of this chapter. I read it to my husband and finished reading as we crossed the Kansas State line. I said, "There! That is the last chapter to this book. I looked over at my husband and found tears streaming down his face. He said, "Honey, how do you know that will be the last chapter?" We both rode along in tears and silence.

Chapter 3

"I Have To Move!!!!"

~Connie~

"I want to move. I can't stay in this house without Lee. Everywhere I look I see him." The days following Lee's death were frustrated with emotion. I wanted to give everything away and move. I made so many decisions so hastily about what to do with Lee's things, that when emotions began to settle down a little, I regretted some of the decisions I had made. We really don't know how we will react in the face of difficult circumstances such as these.

A couple of weeks after Lee's death, I was asking God "Why?". He took me to the scripture, Psalm 116:15, "Precious in the sight of the Lord is the death of His saints." That gave me peace. It's not to say that I wouldn't have days that I still would ask why when it seemed I needed Lee so much, because I did, but God would always bring me back to worship and Psalm 116:15.

Lee was in every part of my life. What am I saying?! Lee was my life! He was my routine. Now, everything about my daily routine and my schedule was gone. My identity had been Mrs. Lee Harris or Mrs. Wal-Mart at the different stores we had managed. Now both identities were gone. I had given my life to Lee and the children. I had no desire to work outside the home. All I wanted was to be a really good wife and mother. Some say I really spoiled Lee. When he came in for lunch, everything was always ready for him and I would bring it to him. I enjoyed waiting on my husband and giving to him. He had given so much to us and he was so dedicated to providing for his family.

Lee's early years in management required keeping a difficult schedule. It called for many weeks without any days off and also long hours. Lee would come home so exhausted he would sleep on his lunch hour and his supper hour. I had to take the children to Wal-Mart for them to see him those first few years, but Lee never complained.

A lot of times, I would feel guilty for staying home with the children while he worked such long, hard hours. I thought many times about going to work, but Lee wanted me to stay home with our children. Even after they were all in school, it was still so important to him that I be home for him and the children. He wanted them to have the best upbringing he could give them, and, to him, that was their mother staying home.

Lee always made sure our children treated me with respect. As David was growing up, he loved to wrestle, and so did I. We would start wrestling, and David would get a little rough. Lee wouldn't say, "David, quit hurting your mother!" He would say, "David, quit hurting my wife!"

The children so enjoyed their father. He was a cool dad. He would let them spend the night with him in Wal-Mart once or twice a year. They could play with anything in the store as long as they put everything back the way they found it and it passed dad's inspection. Their cousins would come down and spend a couple of weeks with us during the summers, and Lee would let them play to their hearts content also. The children so loved those days.

Lee would chase the children around the house, and it would end in big hugs and kisses. There were times I would be out of town, and those were the times he had dates with his daughters. The girls so looked forward to those times. Stacy and Kellie would rearrange their schedules just to have that special dinner with their dad. Father God could not have given us a better husband or father.

He imparted so much into our lives, and showed us what it really meant to live a life of giving. In all the children's growing up years it was always daddy that would give them extra money when they had gone through their allowance. I was the one that always got the new vehicle, and he would make do with what he had.

When Lee died, I was concerned about David. He had been away from God for so long, I didn't know if it would drive him further away or bring him closer. I'm happy to say it brought him closer. After David got home from the funeral, he would call just to talk about the Word of God. God was filling David up with Himself. David was so excited about what God was showing him in the Word. Since his daddy meant everything to him, I have no doubt that it was God's Word that pulled him through his darkest hour.

When Lee accepted his first position as a store manager for Wal-Mart, David was his shadow. We lived right behind the store and every step Lee made, David made it with him. Lee taught him so much. He loved being with his dad. If his daddy couldn't do it, it couldn't be done. David looked to his dad for advice about everything. David was following in his father's footsteps with Wal-Mart, and totally depended on his father for everything he didn't know, and didn't want to ask anybody else. Lee was more than happy to walk him through whatever it was he needed.

I will never forget the last time I saw Lee talk to David over the phone. I was coming into the room when the phone rang and Lee answered it. Lee had been on the edge of his recliner.

A grin came on his face, and he jumped back in the chair like he was going to be talking for a long time. I had to find out to whom he was talking, because I had never before seen Lee react to a phone call like that. As I listened, I could tell it was David. He and David had so much in common, from Wal-Mart to any kind of sports. Lee was an avid golfer and his son was following in his footsteps there also. It gave me such joy to see what an awesome relationship he had with our son. Our God has been so good to our family.

In the earlier chapter I said one of the hardest things I've ever had to do was let David get on that plane following Lee's funeral, but I know it was even harder for him. David has always been so protective of me. He has always made me feel like the most special mother in the world. We would walk through the mall, and at 16 years of age David would have his arm around my shoulders. He was not ashamed of showing his affection, but then, neither was his father.

If David could have gone back home, packed everything up and moved back here, he would have, just to take care of his mom, but he had responsibilities to his own new family. David was just married in the spring of 2001 to his beautiful wife Sandy, and they were making a life of their own. I am so grateful they had each other through this time. He talked to several different men and told them to take care of his mother and sisters for him.

In 2000, I bought Lee a new wedding ring. The one he had worn for 27 years was getting really thin on the edges, and was beginning to cut his finger. We found a ring that we both liked, and we decided that we would make the girls some jewelry out of the ring that I had put on his finger when he was 19. Kellie liked white gold, and Stacy would like anything made out of it just because it was daddy's ring.

Nick proposed to our daughter Kellie at the beginning of 2001. Kellie was so excited, and we now knew what we could do with Lee's wedding ring. We would have earrings made for her to wear on her wedding day. The Monday night before Lee died on Wednesday, we got the earrings from the jeweler. We couldn't decide whether to give them to her right then, or wait until the wedding. We decided to wait until the wedding, but I wish we had given them to her that night. Her daddy would have given them to her, and she would have had that memory. There seems to be quite a few things I would change if I could.

Kellie was Lee's little blued eyed girl. We had taken a picture of Kellie when she was little, and in the picture she had tears in her eyes. It made her eyes so blue. We really don't remember what made her eyes tear up, but Lee loved that picture of her. It would bring such a smile to his face.

Kellie is a very caring, and affectionate person, but very reserved in showing emotion. A lot of times when Kellie was growing up, I wouldn't even know she was angry about something until several different things would happen. Then we all knew Kellie was upset. That is so much like her father. I know it was really hard on Kellie not being able to be with me all the time, and make sure I was okay, but she had a new husband that needed her attention, and that was the best thing for her. Nick's arms helped take her mind off of her daddy not being there.

Stacy was in the process of buying a new car just before her father passed away. Every chance she got; she would talk her daddy into going car shopping with her. The Wednesday before he passed away was one of those days. They decided they would see if they could find something in Wichita. I was out of town, and Stacy was so happy to have her daddy all to herself for the day. He took her to a restaurant of her choosing, and whatever car lot she wanted to go to. She couldn't have asked for a better day. He made her feel so special. But that was Lee Harris. His family was his delight and he made us all feel how special we were to him.

The next best thing to having your spouse's arms to make things better is your daddy's arms. Stacy, our youngest, didn't have either one. Stacy not only lost her dad, but Kellie getting married, and moving out of the house in a few weeks, also caused a void in Stacy's life. Prior to Kellie's wedding, the girls had been able to comfort each other, and talk about daddy without upsetting mother. They didn't want to come to me with their pain, because they thought I was going through too much pain myself. Now Stacy was really lost. She would call the youth Pastor or a couple of other people in our church, and they would talk and pray with her until peace would come, but after a while, she didn't want to impose on anyone, so it got even tougher for her. Finally, she couldn't stand it any longer. She had to have mother's arms. They weren't daddy's arms, but they were the next best thing, and we cried and prayed together.

In a way, I think the grief was harder on Stacy than anyone else. She saw her brother and sister going on with their lives making new families of their own, but she was stuck in her old life, without her father, or a husband to hold her. I was so concerned for my little Stacy. "Please Father God, put Your loving arms around her and heal her hurts."

Lee had been very affectionate with the children and me. Oh, how I missed his hugs. There were times when he would hug me, I would tell him, "Just a little harder please." His arms made me feel so safe. We rarely had a family meal but what we would come together and pray over the meal and after the prayer Lee would give a big group hug before we sat down to eat.

When I was growing up, I never had a lot of self-confidence. When we got married, I still didn't have much, but Lee never put me down for anything. He always encouraged me to be all that I could be. I am so grateful for the man God gave me on this earth. It's not to say that Lee was perfect, but he was as close as it gets on this side of heaven.

He was always doing little things for me. One time when we lived in North Dakota, I had gone on a mission trip to Mexico with our daughters. I had never said anything to Lee about wanting a makeup vanity, but while I was gone he bought one for me and had it set up by the time I got home. I was so surprised since he didn't even know I wanted one. God is so good!

I have always been a very private person never letting a lot of people in my life. Like Lee, as long as I had our family together I really didn't need anybody else, or so I thought. When God started putting Sharolyn and I together, it stirred the waters of our marriage. We had a good marriage, but God was taking us to a deeper level.

Lee had always had all of my attention and it was becoming very apparent to him that he didn't like sharing me. He had never had to share me with anybody and he didn't think he wanted to start now. We had been married for 23 years at that time, and he enjoyed our relationship just the way it was. He wanted me all to himself.

In a "get honest" session, God began to bring a new transparency to our marriage. At first it was difficult for Lee to be transparent and honest with his feelings, and over the years as so many couples do, we had stuffed some of what we were feeling rather than deal with it. It is easier to stuff ugly emotions, hurts, and offences rather than deal with them. It is also easier to go away and deal with it by yourself rather than with your spouse, but these two methods of dealing with offences will begin to clog your love lines. It hurts to show someone else how ugly we are inside. We have to humble ourselves to expose ourselves to another, and our pride doesn't want to do that. We fear rejection, or not being able to measure up, or not being accepted by the other person.

When a relationship fails you can almost always find pride or fear at the root of the separation. Pride and fear will clog your love lines, keeping open and honest communication from flowing. When love lines become clogged, you begin to have no feelings for the other person. It doesn't happen all at once, but like a drain, when you finally get enough debris in there, it's clogged. Unless we become transparent with each other, and confess the hurts, or offences, or ugly emotions, cleansing can't come, and God's grace can't work in our relationship. If we are going to stay in a relationship with another person we must be willing to let God bring our walls down and His grace can do just that. It's only by the grace of God any relationship stays together.

When Lee and I opened up and became transparent with each other, it put us on a whole new level of love. Lee started to romance me again and that was awesome! God made things better than they had ever been before. Lee decided transparency wasn't so bad after all and said, "This is what real love truly is!"

We had such good times in our home, and it was so full of love, it seemed so big and empty without him. During the first month following Lee's death, my desire to move was becoming increasingly more intense. One day Sharolyn called me and asked to come over. When she came in she told me immediately that I wasn't going to enjoy what she had to say, but she felt like she needed to say it. She said she knew I wanted to move and get away, but that wouldn't be the best thing for them or me right now. The children needed to experience the holidays in the stable environment of where their daddy had lived. She was right! I definitely didn't want to hear what she had to say! I really wanted to stomp her foot and dot her eye, but I didn't. I knew what she was saying was right, but it didn't make it any less painful.

Later that same day our oldest daughter Kellie came in and asked if she could talk to me. She asked if we had to move or did I just want to move. I asked her to tell me what she had on her mind. She told me the same thing that Sharolyn had told me hours earlier, so I knew we were supposed to stay in the house. I'm so glad we did. As time went on, staying in that house brought me so much comfort. After I had purchased a house the following June, and it was time to move, I didn't want to. I felt secure in our old home. It was like Lee was still a part of our lives as long as we were there, and I didn't want to lose that.

Even though I still wanted to move during that first month, there was a much more pressing issue at hand. Wedding bells were in the air and there was still much to do, but we had yet another river to cross.

Chapter 4

The River Floods Again

~Sharolyn~

In August of 2001, Jerry and I were sitting on our deck at home when Jerry became very serious. He said, "Sharolyn, I feel like we are going to have a major change in the fall." I quizzed him as to what he thought that meant. He didn't know but he just knew in his heart we would have a major change.

I had entered a Master's degree program at a university in Oklahoma City in September, and the first class was the week of 9/11. The whole country was in turmoil. We had a service the evening of 9/11 for the college students, and two people gave me words of exhortation. Both words had to do with change. One was a geographical change and the other was a change of ministry. I called home and told my husband that maybe our major change was a move. All of that kind of thinking was totally forgotten when Lee died the very next week. Lee's death was enough of a major change in all of our lives.

Jerry had enrolled in August to attend a training seminar the last of September to learn concrete stamping. After Lee died, he almost cancelled his enrollment, but after much deliberation he decided to attend the seminar. He came back so excited at the potential of beginning a part-time business. This would be a major change for us, so we thought maybe that was what Jerry had sensed in August. Then Wednesday night, October 3rd, just prior to service, Jerry came to the stage where I was playing the keyboard preparing for the worship service. The gas utility company he had worked for the last 20 years had announced that day a merger was in process. If we were going to stay with our company, we would have to move. That is quite a piece of news to receive prior to being a part of leading the congregation into worship. My mind was reeling. How could this be? I can't leave Connie now! Lee's dead! Kellie is getting married! What was going on? Suddenly, it felt like nothing was stable.

Jerry and I have always been pretty stable people. We lived 19 years in the same house after marriage. We had only moved one time and that was just 13 miles into the country from the first home. Jerry had the same job 20 years. I had worked as an associate pastor at the same church for 11 years. We definitely did not fall into the average stats of the mobile society we live in. Jerry's parents lived 30 minutes away and my parents lived 15 minutes away. This was important because all of our parents were well over 80 years of age. Jerry's parents had two other children living close by, but my parents had no one else close by to look after them. What would my parents do if we were to move away?

Connie, on the other hand, moved 9 times in 27 years. Lee would get promoted to another store and they would be moved within two weeks of notification. For Connie and Lee, moving was a new adventure with new people to meet, but this proposed move for Jerry and I rattled everyone's timbers, including Connie and her family. We can't be moving at a time like this!

October 17th was a brisk, fall morning. Jerry and Brian, our 15 year old son, left for school around 6 A.M. in their little blue Chevy Sprint. It was Wednesday four weeks to the day of Lee's death. Brian had an early morning weight lifting class for football. Brian was accumulating hours on his restricted license, so he was in the driver's seat. It was dark. Sunrise wouldn't happen until 7:40 A.M. that morning. Lights were turned on and the trip was in process. A little more than 5 miles from our home a 1-ton Dodge pickup was approaching an upcoming intersection from the south. The pickup was controlled by a stop sign. Brian and Jerry were traveling on a 55 m.p.h. county road with no traffic control signs. By the time Brian saw the pickup was not going to stop, even though 60 feet of skid marks were laid, there was no way he could avoid hitting the pickup. The time was 6:13 A.M.

Jonathan, our 12 year old, and I were traveling the same

road an hour and a half later when we began to see daddy's car parked in the North ditch. Jon and I began to wonder why daddy had parked his car in such a strange place. You could see the car more than a half-mile away and it looked okay from the rear. The closer we got we could see the highway patrol that were still there investigating the accident. Then we saw the front of the car. There was nothing left on the passenger's side. I stopped the car while they were waving us on, and said, "That is my husband's car! Where is my family?"

We were told Brian had been taken by ground ambulance to Hutchinson Hospital, and Jerry had been airlifted to St. Francis in Wichita. They would not tell me the condition of either of them. Jonathan and I got back in our car completely overwhelmed. We headed for Wichita, as I knew Jerry must be the most serious. As Jon and I were leaving the scene of the accident traveling to Wichita, officers from the scene were knocking on the front door of our home waking our oldest son, Nathan, telling him the news. I saw patrol cars as I turned the corner a little more than a mile from our house, but I had no idea they were looking for my family.

~Connie~

Sharolyn called me on her cell phone and screamed that Jerry and Brian had been in a car accident. I told her I would go to the Hutchinson hospital to be with Brian. In my heart, I felt like everything would be all right. People have accidents all the time and they are fine. Besides, we had just lost Lee and God definitely would not let us lose Jerry also. When I got to the hospital in Hutchinson, they were transferring Brian to Wichita. I was so glad we could be with Sharolyn. I could imagine what she was going through.

-Sharolyn-

We arrived at the hospital and the first thing they wanted was paperwork while my only thought was *I have to see my husband.* Still, no one would tell me anything. When the hospital chaplain was the first one to come to me, I knew things weren't good. They told me to wait outside of a treatment room door and when they came out to go to the ICU, I could see my husband. He was unconscious, his face was swollen, but he was still alive. Jerry was placed immediately on life support as he had such extensive injuries both internally and externally.

Brian was transferred to St. Francis due to head injuries he had suffered. I was relieved to know he would be in the same hospital with his dad instead of 50 miles away. He was admitted to the pediatric floor of the hospital, which was quite a distance from Jerry's room, but they were in the same hospital and for that I was grateful.

Jerry's vital signs had to be maintained by IV drips. As the vitals would lower more IV therapy would be given. Until they had come to the limit to which they could give the drugs. There seemed to be no separation of days. People would come and go. Many, many friends came and some stayed constantly with me. Connie rarely left my side. How could this be happening? We had just buried Lee days before. Now the life of my husband was also threatened.

Several months before the accident, Jerry received a word in a prayer line at our church saying he would live and not die and declare the glory of God in the earth. We came home wondering what that had meant but over time we had forgotten about the word. While we were in the hospital, that was recalled to mind and we believed that the word must have been spoken for this time. Our belief was he would live and not die. I knew he would make it. Surely we would not lose both Lee and Jerry.

Prayer was going up continually. We just knew that God was greater than this. It would seem like Jerry would get better and we would rejoice. When he would get worse we knew God was greater. We stayed at the hospital constantly. We slept there, ate there, lived there. We didn't want to leave his side. When he woke up, we wanted to be there. He was going to wake up! One night, everyone encouraged me to leave the hospital and stay at a room we had been given in the Ronald McDonald house. I went to the room and it was the longest, loneliest hours of the entire stay in the hospital. I had to get back to the hospital.

Our church and our friends from the community where my children attend school were so wonderful. Different ones would bring just what we needed when we needed it. They cared for my children. They dug deep into their pockets providing phone cards, cash, and even warm soft blankets for those moments we could rest. Some things are such a blur that we don't even know what all was given and done, but we know we were taken care of very well. I remembered our boat was to go in for winterization and a dear church member instantly said, "I'll handle it." We were so thankful that we were a part of the body of Christ. We don't know what we would have done without them. We knew they were praying when we couldn't.

Brian was dismissed Friday evening only having to stay in the hospital a couple of days. God was so gracious to us. He would be scarred, but fine! After Brian was dismissed, the pace of running between rooms stopped, but soon the activity in my husband's room picked up. He was on everything imaginable to keep him alive. The bed Jerry was on rotated from side to side continually to aid with circulation. The ventilator and IV drips were constant. If the nursing staff failed to change the drips immediately as they emptied, Jerry's vital signs would drop. We kept a CD of worship music playing continuously in his room. The nursing staff was so good to let me come in all the time unless they were tending to Jerry's needs even though we were in ICU.

Many times vitals were looking like things were improving. How encouraging that improvement was, but then it was said surgery would have to be done and more aggressive means taken to hold our ground. His abdominal cavity was becoming distended from escaping gases and air. Was I willing for them to do surgery to relieve the pressure and reduce his stress elevation? Yes, by all means I was willing if it would give us more time to get our miracle. They did the surgery and we were told all went well. We may have a fighting chance. Time would tell.

Jerry's brother-in-law had a vision while praying during the time we were waiting in ICU. The vision was of a pole connecting Jerry's shoulder to my shoulder and precious fruit was being carried between us. Our interpretation of the vision was Jerry's brush with death would allow him to see things in heaven. Jerry would live and not die and would bring "fruit" from heaven to share with us.

Sunday many of the church people came to see us. Some of us went to the chapel at the hospital and took communion and sang some worship songs. One member brought a drum. I love the drums. I could feel the presence of the Lord in our worship and it strengthened me. We came back to ICU and continued to wait.

Sunday evening things were not looking good. Medications were no longer working and there was no more to give. Later Sunday night I was asked to make the decision to take Jerry off of life support. The doctors said there was nothing more they could do. They would be back for my decision. I could not make that decision. I knew what they were saying, but I could not make that decision. We knew he would live and not die. They called us into the family room. It looked like the end was near, but this can't be happening again!

Before the doctors returned to ask my decision, the nurses called us to come to Jerry's room. They said it was time to say goodbye as he was dying. His heart was slowing and the vitals were dropping. Every monitor in his room was dropping and there was absolutely nothing we could do but watch. With my hand on his heart it beat for the last time at 52 minutes after midnight October 22, 2001. My strength left me! My best friend, the love of my life of 22 years was gone!

Those in the room helped me back to the family room. Our children and Connie didn't make it to the room before Jerry died. Jonathan had continued to say, "My daddy won't die. He is too stubborn to die." But now we had to look in the eyes of three young men, 19, 15, and 12 years of age and say your dad didn't make it. The anguish! Lee and Jerry's deaths were only 33 days apart. The grief over losing Lee was still so raw and exposed. Now both of our men were gone. Words can't express the compounded grief we both felt in the moments that followed.

~Connie~

Our pastor took Sharolyn, the boys and I to Sharolyn's house. I spent the night with her. Sharolyn cried herself to sleep. I would awaken all during the night and find her crying. She would cry for a while and sleep for a while. When morning finally came, Sharolyn woke up in a black hole of grief. Her cries were that of deep groans of anguish, hardly able to catch her breath. That really scared me, and I didn't know what to do. I was praying in the spirit big time, but I felt like I really needed help. As soon as I could, I called a good friend of ours and told her what was happening and asked her to pray also. I was afraid we would lose her in that black hole of grief. God heard and answered our prayers and gave her peace.

Chapter 5

What Happened?!

~Sharolyn~

Questions! There were so many questions from within and without. Of course, Monday morning my family was at the mortuary. I had just been here with Connie. Now she was here with me, and the same people were asking the same questions. Where would he be buried? When do you want to have the service? Where will you have the service? What coffin do you want? What size was Jerry while he was alive? I discovered I needed to buy a new suit two sizes larger for burial as he was so swollen from the blunt force injuries. We had a very private viewing for immediate family the night before the funeral. We could not have an open casket. Over a thousand people were at his funeral. He was a very quiet steady man, but oh, the number of lives he had touched.

All who came to Lee and Jerry's funerals said they had never experienced anything like their services. There was such worship to the Father in both services. Jerry had given me fresh flowers every Friday for eight years. At the end of the service all the people came one by one to greet the boys and me. Pastor had purchased fresh flowers for all the men to give me as they passed by. By the time I had greeted all who had come, there were fresh flowers everywhere around me.

In the days that followed, my heart was full of questions. Jerry was supposed to live and not die. "God, what happened?" I was so focused on his living that dying was totally out of the question. Have you ever attended a rodeo and watched the calf-roping event? I was feeling like the calf. I had been running headlong down the field expecting to get to the other end with Jerry receiving a miraculous recovery when, like the calf, the rope of reality hit my neck, throwing me to the ground. It took my breath away. I felt like I was staggering to get back up and disoriented as to even know where the other end was anymore. We were all stunned. All became quiet.

Where there were words of hope and faith, silence descended. Grief descended upon the church. No one knew what to say anymore. This just didn't seem to fit with all the faith teaching and belief system in place in our minds and hearts. If Connie and I said it once we said it a hundred times, "I can't get my mind around this!"

Connie and I are both praying women and we have had

answers to prayer when the odds seemed impossibly high against the answer coming. Many times before and since the deaths of our husbands, the Holy Spirit has prayed through us to accomplish His purpose. We both have been moved to pray at different times in our lives, and knew that danger had been avoided for our families. Where was the urge to pray on the morning of the accident? Where was the urge to pray on the morning of Lee's heart attack? Some people told me they were awakened to pray for Jerry the morning of the accident. *"God! Where was I?"*

I was tidying up the house and getting Jon ready for school doing normal routine stuff. I had no clue my family had crashed five miles away. Connie and I were praying over whether to exchange a ring or not when Lee had his heart attack.

Two off-time deaths of outstanding men who were the best of friends dying 33 days apart jolted the people of the church. Some judgment surfaced but it wasn't anything that we had not questioned ourselves. "If you would have had enough faith, Lee and Jerry would not have died." "You must have opened a door somewhere for the enemy to attack you." We were asking ourselves the same questions, "Why didn't we have enough faith, and have we opened a door somewhere?"

One Sunday morning during service Connie and I could sense such judgment we wanted to crawl in a hole and never surface again. Our pastor sensed it also and immediately began to address it from the pulpit.   Specifically by name, our pastor called Connie and I to the front to help with the altar ministry. It wasn't unusual for me to help with altar ministry as I was a pastor and elder of the church, but he had never called Connie specifically by name before. We felt the anointing of the Lord come on us for ministry and in that instant we felt the judgments lift that were being inflicted by others and ourselves.

We began ministering together down the prayer line. I moved on ahead of Connie to another person leaving her praying for the last person. Suddenly, I felt the anointing lift. In my heart I questioned what was going on. I had prayed for people many times alone before. God spoke in my heart that He had called Connie and me to work together as a team. I went back to where Connie was praying and again felt the anointing for ministry.

The word that sustained us through all of this time was the word God spoke in Connie's heart a week after Lee's death. "This is not about you. It is not about your pain. It is about Me and My glory." Now Connie and I were both faced with the question, *How do we continue to walk in the midst of the most devastating unanswered prayers of our lives and bring Him glory?*

My first experience with believing God for something major and it not coming to pass in my family was December of 1999. My family believed God for a miracle for my 31 year old niece who had been diagnosed with cancer earlier in the year.

The day she died Connie and I had been fasting and praying for her healing and suddenly we felt a release in our spirits. We just knew she was healed. In a few minutes I received the call that Kristy had died at the very time we had received the release in our spirits from prayer. She was healed but in the wrong realm in my way of thinking. I wanted her healed this side of glory. She was only 31 years old, had never been married, and was a good Christian woman. *Why did she have to die?*

My faith began teetering over what seemed to be a great divide. What I had been taught and had lived all of my life didn't seem to be working. Instead of shouting victory over death, I was preaching a funeral. Obviously there was an element to faith I did not yet understand.

What went wrong? I was shaken to the very core of my being, but in the midst of that shaking, God began talking to me about His Sovereignty. It began to come out of my spirit that God was Sovereign, even when I didn't understand the circumstances or what "sovereign" really meant.

Connie and I had questions for God and He had questions for us. Would we still love Him even if things did not turn out according to our expectations? Would we trust Him to be God in the midst of circumstances and outcomes that we could not understand? Would we be dependent upon His grace regardless? These questions could not be answered with a quick yes or no.

These answers had to be walked out in real life. We could not say we loved or trusted God if we could not worship Him in the midst of circumstances beyond our control.

Sometimes we say we walk by faith when actually we have been able to strategically manipulate circumstances or portfolios to continue to give us what we want. If plan "A" fails we have plan "B". But when plan "A" and plan "B" dies, what do you do? Our experience is: it's a lot easier to believe God for something and get it, than to believe God for something and not get it and have to walk out the loss by faith. In this confusion is where a lot of Christians lose it.

Connie and I had been leading a prayer group on Tuesday nights. The Tuesday before the accident I told the few that were there praying, "I see me taking a step. My foot is in the air, but I don't know where to put it down." What I didn't know was the very next morning I would also be launched into the same world with Connie and the only way we could live it would be by a deeper revelation of faith than we currently knew. The level of faith we knew was where our foot had been standing, but God was about to teach us where to put our other foot.

Connie and I had been dropped into the same river of widowhood 33 days apart. We had no clue where the river was taking us. We just knew we were in it together, but now Kellie's wedding was only 21 days away.

Chapter 6

"Well I'm On!"

~Sharolyn~

It was a blessing to have wedding plans pressing. Wedding preparations were healthy distractions giving brief intermissions from grief. But even in the midst of wedding plans there was the nagging question, "Why could Lee not have given his daughter away and why was Jerry gone too?"

We can only imagine what our children were going through during this time. The girls had just lost their father and needed their mother, but we were day and night at the hospital with Jerry. Our boys had just lost their second dad, and were now threatened with the loss of their own father. The wedding was drawing nearer. Emotions were swirling.

I will never forget Kellie's face when she gave me a beautiful picture with a poem entitled God's Promise after Jerry died. It reads like this: "God didn't promise days without pain, Joy without sorrow, or sun without rain. But, God did promise strength for the day, comfort for tears and a light for the way. And for those who believe in His kingdom of love, He answers their faith with His peace from above." Much prayer was going up that the wedding would be a joyous occasion, not shrouded with grief, and it certainly was a joyous occasion with His peace from above.

~Connie~

The day of the wedding was here before we knew it. Kellie was so excited about getting married but was so sad that her daddy would not be there to give her away. We all had such mixed emotions, but we knew God's grace would see us through. It just had to! David and Sandy flew in from Utah and David gave his sister away. David was such a tower of strength. It felt good to have his arms around us. He and Sandy brought such joy into our home.

Our church family rallied around us. They did everything they could to make Kellie and Nick's wedding the most wonderful day. Stacy was Kellie's maid of honor. Our daughters were so beautiful. Their father would have been so proud of them. Lee always thought he had the most beautiful girls in the world. "Lee where are you? I am so hurting without you here with me. Kellie is so beautiful and we all need your loving arms around us right now."

We placed a table in honor of Lee off to the side at the

front of the church with a picture of Kellie in her father's embrace. As she came down the isle I looked at her and then back at the picture. Tears fell because she was so beautiful and her father wasn't there with us, but by God's grace, joy came that day.

Nick had a lapel microphone so the congregation could hear Nick and Kellie say their vows. Our pastor's microphone wasn't on for the first few minutes. Nick told his dad, "Well, I'm on," and everyone cracked up with laughter. When pastor asked Kellie if she would receive Nick as her husband, she leaned forward over into the microphone on Nick's lapel and said, "I do" and again laughter filled the room.

Nick prepared a video ahead of time that was hilarious. When pastor asked for the ring, no one had it. All the groomsmen asked the next one in line until they came to Nick's youngest brother. He exited the church on the run slamming through the sanctuary doors then the video picked up. The video showed him running across the parking lot, up the driveway to his home, down the stairs, into his room, pulling open a drawer, and throwing clothes everywhere until he found the little black box. Out of the room he ran, back up the stairs, down the driveway, across the parking lot, and back into the church where he literally came busting through the sanctuary doors and dragged himself huffing and puffing up the isle gripping the little black box in his hand. It passed up through the groomsmen and was handed to Pastor. When he opened the box it contained a Lego piece. Laughter descended on the house, the real ring was produced, and the wedding was a wonderful event. God was so good! But now the wedding was over. The push of adrenaline needed for the wedding day was over. Again there was a closure and a void. The desire I previously felt to move to another house resurfaced even stronger.

Chapter 7

Paint the Fence White

~Sharolyn~

Connie and I reacted to the deaths of our husbands as opposite as we have reacted to everything else. Connie wanted to move and move she did to a very nice home she purchased a few blocks away from the home where they lived at the time of Lee's death. She moved the first weekend of June of 2002. That gave her new inspiration to shop. She had a house to decorate and furnish. There were little remodeling projects that also needed attention, so that was right down my alley. Many of our church family questioned if I would move, but I never had a desire to move. I needed projects.

The most important project pressing on my mind as soon as Kellie was married was painting the 3-foot fence surrounding my patio and front yard white. It felt like a demand inside of me to paint it white. Other things would take my time, or the wind would be blowing, and I was becoming frustrated at not being able to get that fence painted. Several people, including Connie, couldn't understand why I had to paint that fence white. It was a weathered cedar fence and really didn't need painting. I didn't know why I had to paint that fence either, but within six weeks after Jerry's death I was attempting to paint.

Jerry had an airless sprayer, so I bought two huge buckets of white paint and got to work. I poured the paint in the sprayer and turned it on. The sprayer spit globs of paint at the fence. It became an incredible mess. I took the sprayer apart and put it back together two or three times, and it still wouldn't work. By this time, there was a lot of paint on me and globs on the fence resembling modern art. That wasn't quite the effect I had in mind.

Frustration had set in. Jerry would have known what to do. The overwhelming feeling of, *what am I going to do without him?*, descended upon me again as it so often had since the day of his death. I cried out in tears, "Jerry, what do I do?" My eyes fell immediately on a knob I had not noticed before that moment. I turned the knob, and the little machine started spraying away. Then I couldn't paint because I couldn't see the fence for the tears.

The vision my brother-in-law had of a pole being connected from Jerry's shoulder to my shoulder bearing precious fruit came instantly back to my mind. At that moment, I had the sense that Jerry and I were still connected. Please do not misunderstand me. I do not believe in talking to the dead or praying to the dead. We are connected in the sense that Jerry's faith is not complete without mine and mine is not complete without his.

Hebrews 12:1 says we are surrounded by "a great cloud of witnesses" cheering us on. I've known that all my life. I have just never known anyone as intimately as I knew my husband in that cloud before. I had to laugh because I could just imagine the cloud of witnesses watching my painting experience, clapping and saying, "She did it!" More importantly, they are lending their faith to ours cheering us on to complete the course that has been set before us with patient endurance and steady persistence. They have borne testimony to the Truth throughout their lives. How can we do any less? "So let us throw off the weights of sin that distracts us from Jesus the author and the finisher of our faith." Hebrews 12: 1-2

That little episode with the paint sprayer made me know that God would take care of us. After I painted the fence white, I discovered the light from my kitchen window would illuminate off the white fence bringing light into the darkness of my mornings. That gave me a sense of warmth and comfort in the mornings. Having to get up alone in the country in complete darkness where there are no street lights had been depressing without my husband. That simple little fence saved me from thoughts of depression. It was no wonder I had to paint the fence white.

Project after project would come to my mind to do. I threw myself into a flurry of work. If I hurt myself or my muscles ached, that was okay too, because for a little while the physical pain would take my mind off of the emotional pain of the loss of Jerry and Lee. If Connie and I weren't working at my house, we were working on hers. Many times I have looked to the heavens and thanked my heavenly Father for all the remodeling, repairing, and maintenance experiences I had with my husband of 22 years. I had no idea I was being equipped by those experiences for this time in my life, but there are always those things one is unable to do alone.

God gave Connie and I both a very special couple in our church that continued to cover us and walk with us after our husbands died. So many things were completed at my home because of their assistance and every week without fail Connie's lawn would be taken care of. They prayed and called almost daily to check on us. We don't know what we would have done without them.

We both felt like our husbands were just gone on a trip and they would return soon. There seemed to be an internal clock that would go off inside of us when it should have been time for our men to get home from work, and we would expect them to walk through the door only to remember they were never coming home again. Years of habits are not easily changed, but when a key player is taken from the mix everything changes instantly. Our minds and emotions weren't so quick to make the change. We both just wanted to run away.

Chapter 8

The God of a Second Pizza

~Sharolyn~

It was amazing how God began to lead us to different passages of scripture or a paragraph in a book that would encourage our hearts or bring understanding to us. One such scripture leaped off the page found in Habakkuk 3:17-19 (Amplified):

> "Though the fig tree does not blossom and there is no fruit on the vines, (though) the product of the olive fails and the fields yield no food, though the flock is cut off from the fold and there are no cattle in the stalls, yet I will rejoice in the Lord; I will exult in the (victorious) God of my salvation! The Lord God is my Strength, my personal bravery, and my invincible army; He makes, my feet like hinds' feet and will make me to walk (not to stand still in terror, but to walk) and make (spiritual) progress upon my high places (of trouble, suffering, or responsibility)!"

Connie and I could relate to the first part of this passage of scripture. It seemed our lives had been turned upside down. The employment our families had been used to was no longer available. Everything we had become accustomed to having changed. It really felt like we were experiencing no blossoms or fruit and two members of our flock had definitely been "cut off" from our fold. We felt so inept at managing our homes without our husbands.

The prophet Habakkuk says regardless of all these things "I will rejoice in the Lord; I will exult in the victorious God of my salvation!" It rose up in our spirit that this was a choice. We can either choose to pity ourselves for the calamity we find ourselves in or we can choose to rejoice in the midst of our calamity. We chose to rejoice and exult the victorious God of our salvation. Many times our rejoicing was with many tears. That sounds like a paradox, but at times we could not help the emotions we were feeling but we could choose our will. So our choice was, "We will rejoice regardless."

With the prophet we echoed the last part of the verse declaring God to be our strength, personal bravery and invincible army. We declared our feet would be like hinds' feet, and that we would walk and not stand still in terror. It is so easy when we experience an extreme hit to succumb to fear and stand still in terror. This scripture said we would make spiritual progress in the midst of trouble, suffering, or responsibility.

The way the Amplified phrased this portion accurately described the circumstances we were in. We were definitely in a troubled time, suffering, and the responsibility of managing our homes, becoming the heads of our households, was great. That really hit us when the IRS reclassified us from "Married, Filing Jointly" to "Single, Head of Household."

We had to produce death certificates for every legal paper we owned. The process was long and arduous to change everything from and/or to single ownership. Some things fell through the cracks and surfaced months later demanding they be taken care of to suffice legalities. The household management decisions that were seemingly effortless when shared by two now became mountainous. The pressure of full responsibility for all decisions was tremendous. Habakkuk said we would walk and make progress in the midst of the responsibility, suffering, and trouble. He also said God would be our strength, personal bravery, and invincible army.

Connie and I had leaned into our husbands for their strength, personal bravery, and if need be we felt like they could become an invincible army. Now we found ourselves dealing with people and things that would have been our husbands' role. We certainly needed God's strength and personal bravery. Sometimes the things we would find ourselves having to do for our households were intimidating to us as women, and we felt like we needed an invincible army. We began feeling inside of ourselves that we were making progress not only spiritually, but also in managing our households, and our dependency was definitely upon God to be our Father, our husband, and the Father to our children.

My two younger children had spring break in March of 2002. Connie and I decided we would take Brian and Jonathan to Branson, Missouri. Nathan, my oldest son, was in college and lived on a completely different schedule or he would have gone also. It was so good to get away and just enjoy some of the shows there.

Jonathan is always hungry. One night at 10:00 he wanted a pizza. None of the rest of us were hungry, so I called in an order at the nearest Pizza Hut for a small, deep-pan, pepperoni pizza. When I arrived, the man was cutting it up behind the counter. All the while he was cutting and boxing, he called my attention to how beautiful the pizza was and that he had put "double" toppings on it. I thanked him and told him he certainly didn't have to do that. I paid for the pizza and went out to my car. As I put my hand on the door, the man called to me from the door of the Pizza Hut, "Sharolyn. Come back in here. I have something for you." Talk about startled! Nobody knew me in Branson, and this man was calling my name? I then remembered I gave my name when I called the pizza order in from the motel, but the strange part was he even pronounced it right. No one does that!

I followed him into the Pizza Hut and waited at the counter. He began to talk to another man behind the counter about a medium, deep-pan, pepperoni pizza that had just come out of the oven. The other man told him who the pizza was for, but the man who knew my name said, "Make them another. This pizza is going to the lady." Now Pizza Hut normally doesn't make a practice of giving pizzas away, especially when the 2nd pizza is larger than the one you paid for. I accepted the pizza and thanked the man again wondering just what had happened.

When I arrived at the motel, Connie saw me walk in with two pizza boxes. "Two pizzas? What on earth for?" I told her the story as to what had happened and tears came to both of our eyes at the same time. We had been praying Isaiah 54 that God would be our husband as He had promised to be the husband to the widow and the Father to our children. The man had put "double" toppings on my son's pizza. But he also gave us a second pizza at no cost. God was showing us he would take care of our children and bless them with a double portion, but that he would also bless us, His wife. The very next week, Connie was given an unexpected financial bonus that blessed her, and enabled her to bless her children. Since then we have reminded ourselves when things look rough, "He is the God of a second pizza."

Chapter 9

See You at the Crossroads

~Sharolyn~

The hit tune "See You at the Crossroads" played over and over in Brian's room. That song seemed to speak to his heart, probably because the story of the song was so similar to his own. It was at the crossroads the two vehicles met on that fateful day.

Not long after Jerry died, I went up to Brian's room but he was not there. It was a cold, dark night, "See You at the Crossroads" was playing in his boom box, his window was wide open, and the screen was setting inside on the floor. He had gone out of his 2nd story window, and was sitting on the roof of the porch. I climbed out on the roof, sat down beside him, and held him. Tears gushed and he began to talk. He began to tell of all he had experienced at the scene of the accident. I could only imagine the horror he experienced that morning in the darkness before sunrise.

Brian did not know how he got out of the car, but

remembered wandering around outside it. He heard his dad struggling to breath and once dad stopped breathing. He shook his dad and he started breathing again. He didn't know what to do before the EMS arrived, so he lay down on the pavement beside his dad who was still penned in the car and listened for him to breathe.

Brian was so angry with the other driver. "Why didn't he stop, Mom? There was nothing I could do." We talked through it not being Brian's fault. We talked and cried through our loss and our pain. We talked until we could say no more. We were both shaking from the cold. The cold seemed to be as much inside of us as outside that night. All we could do was cry out to God for help, the grief was so great. We have continued to talk out the anger and pray for God's peace and comfort. Everyone, I am sure, has been guilty of rolling through a stop sign occasionally. It doesn't make us bad people, but it sure can cost a life and that loss is great. We crawled back through the window and headed for the couch, Brian laid his head in my lap. When our children were little and they would get hurt, they would climb up in either mommy or daddy's lap. Our arms were such a refuge to them and the kisses would somehow make it go away. With Brian's head in my lap, I began to pray, "Father, this family is crawling up into your lap. Please hold us and kiss us and make the grief go away."

Jerry was one of those remarkable fathers. Whatever his

children were interested in, he was interested in. Brian was big into football and Jerry would take off work early to make it to the distant games. He never missed a game. Brian was a good player, carrying the ball more than 170 yards in one game. He knew no pain and would hit hard. His dad was so proud of him. I don't know much about the sport of football, so I asked Brian, "What does the team do if their star player is hurt and taken out of the game before the game is over?" Brian said, "We roll over and keep playing the best we can." I said, "Then Brian, we are going to roll over and do the best we can without our star player to finish our game."

It takes faith to walk where you have not walked before. It takes faith to become a new family unit. We have become dependant on the grace of God to see us through all of the adjustments since Jerry died. It takes faith to allow the Holy Spirit to speak words through you that will help and not hinder the healing of emotions. It takes more faith to pray for a miracle and not get it than to pray for a miracle and get it and then it is over. It takes faith to learn to live again in a new life, and not become bitter. Day in and day out the loss of Jerry and Lee is in our face one way or another.

Connie and I and my three sons went on a two-week road trip to California the summer after Jerry and Lee's death. Two days into the trip my family was at each other as only families can do. Nobody could do anything to please anyone. I knew it was to a great degree because dad wasn't with us, and we were going it alone for the first time. We sat down in the motel room and began to discuss again what it meant to be a new family nucleus. It wasn't anything great I said, but it was the great grace of God that began to pour into that room that took the anger away. He became the father to my children in that room and a new respect for every member of the family came over us. Until that moment, I was ready to turn the car around and go back home. But after that moment, we had a wonderful trip.

Both of our families had to deal with anger. All of us were angry at one time or another. I am just grateful God's grace kept us all from being angry at the same time. We were angry at the man for running the stop sign. We were angry that the doctor who did Lee's physical had not found the weakness in Lee's heart. We were angry with Lee and Jerry for dying. We were angry at being robbed of our husbands, fathers, nurturers, counselors, providers, and caregivers.

We were lost. How do we continue without the strength and support of our men? I officially quit my position at the church January 1 of 2002. I actually never went back to work after Jerry's death. My children weren't grown and we had to learn to be a family again. There had to be security and stability in our home. Jerry had provided that before the accident. He literally supported all of the rest of us in our endeavors. We really didn't understand how much he supported all of us, and was the anchor of our home until he was gone.

Nathan, our oldest son, had a passion for animals. He and his dad were in the midst of a goat project when Jerry was killed. They would go to animal auctions together to buy, sell, or just hang out. I'll never forget the time Jerry got a call from Nathan the weekend prior to the wreck. Jerry hung up the phone grinning from ear to ear. Nathan had tied a load of "stuff" on our pickup but in the process had somehow tied the doors shut to the cab of the truck. He couldn't get out unless he climbed through the window, which would be pretty embarrassing because people were watching. Thank God for cell phones and a Dad to the rescue.

Nathan still had fence to build and many things to learn that his father would have been right there with him all the way. I suppose we were a motley crew, but all of the boys and I began to help Nathan in his endeavor. It took all of us to take dad's place on building the fence, but building it was yet another step in teaching us to pull together as a family. It wasn't that any of the rest of us enjoyed the goats. Quite the contrary, but Nathan had a need, and we pulled together as a family. In working together, the boys gained more respect for the other's strengths and abilities. We discovered we needed each other as we learned to relate together differently than before. Where we all leaned into dad before, we had to learn to lean into each other.

Brian's passion was mechanics. Brian and his dad had made it a summer project to get the Chevy Sprint back on the road after a short retirement. It had been Jerry's work car, but when the starter went out among other things, he decided he would rather drive a truck. Brian was already showing aspirations of driving a stick shift, so we kept the Sprint to give to Brian to drive as his school car. By the time school started, the car was ready to go, and Brian had a taste of mechanics. Nathan always leaned into dad for help on his car. He discovered he could lean into Brian for mechanical things. Brian has grown in his mechanical ability because of being needed. Nathan is quick to tell me when we need something mechanical done or welding done, "Oh Brian can do that." What a confidence builder to be acknowledged for your skill like that by your older brother.

Jonathan was only 12 years old when his daddy died. Dad and Jonathan shared cooking and canning. Yes canning! Jerry was a hot sauce addict who taught the rest of us to love hot sauce. He raised his own tomatoes and jalapeno peppers. Jonathan and his dad would can it in quart jars. Only Jon knew his dad's "secret recipe." The night before the accident Jerry was canning hot sauce. I came in that night about 10 o'clock. Three steps inside the house tears began coming to my eyes. "Honey, did you put any tomatoes in this batch of hot sauce?" It was the end of the season and it was nearly all jalapeno peppers.

When people began coming to my house the day of the

funeral, I put a bowl of the last batch of hot sauce Jerry had made on the table. I warned everyone it was hot. Connie still tried to use it as a chip dip. There were people everywhere, and Connie started hooting and hollering, climbing over people to the water. What a commotion! I got so tickled; I had to laugh. Jerry was such a quiet prankster, and that would have made his day.

It seems there is this day that comes in a young man's life that his maleness awakens in him and then he becomes dad's young man instead of so much mamma's little boy. Jon is just now awakening. My heart aches for Jon because he is not enjoying this awakening with his father. Just the other day, Jonathan and I had a strong discussion over him not wanting to attend Brian's spring concert. It is amazing to me how many times I have thought I was addressing one issue, only to find that the issue at hand was covering up the real issue.

Jon didn't want to go to the concert because he thought that no one cared about him. Mom was the only one who really loved him in the family so far as he was concerned. His brothers only did things with him when they had to. Red flags went up. Jon now was in need of that male support. His complaints were valid. The other boys only took him places if they wanted or needed to go. He was getting the idea what he wanted and needed didn't matter to them. It was time for another chat with the older boys. God's grace came through again. Nathan and Brian caught immediately that Jon needed "big brothers."

Brian is teaching Jon how to change oil and other "stuff." Brian came in the house just the other morning saying, "Mom you can't believe how well Jon is doing changing the oil." Jon came in covered from head to toe with oil, but grinning from ear to ear. Nathan is spending time with Jon on his days off. God's grace is seeing us through as a team, not just as individual players. I am so grateful. We need each other and we are not so proud that we can't say, "I need you."

Chapter 10

A Dozen Red Roses
Minus One

First occasions and important days after losing a spouse are hard to endure such as that first date, or when he asked you to marry him, or birthdays, holidays, and all those other special events that only two lovers share. We made the trip back to Lee's grave in Arkansas in April. On the way there, we stopped to pick out the stone for Lee's grave. Connie chose the stone and the wording and began to write the check for the purchase and the date washed over her. That day would have been Lee and Connie's 28th wedding anniversary. More tears fell. "What am I doing picking out a headstone for my anniversary?"

We traveled on to the cemetery. I stayed in the car so Connie could have time alone at the grave. As with everything in Arkansas, the grave was over the hill. In minutes, Connie was back up the hill and at the car. Her tears had become intense anger. The grave was awful. Nothing more had been done to it since the day of the funeral when Connie's brothers had filled it in with a shovel.

We went to the only store in the community and asked about the groundskeeper, and how we could contact him, only to discover he had been gone on an "extended" vacation. Connie was beside herself. I knew we could not leave things as we had found them for her well-being.

We went back to the cemetery and found a house across the road where we could borrow a shovel and a wheelbarrow. We shoveled, smoothed, and mounded the grave the best we could. It actually looked pretty good by the time we were done. Then we gathered rocks and placed them around the perimeter of the grave. Connie was eased and again I left her alone.

Connie and I both were in a maze of tombstones on our wedding anniversaries following the death of our husbands. I had chosen Jerry's stone in March. It should have been set in May or June but it wasn't set until what would have been our 23rd wedding anniversary in September. It seemed so strange for Connie to be purchasing and me to be receiving stones for our anniversaries the year following our husbands' deaths.

Jerry's birthday rolled around. It happened to fall on a Wednesday night and I was at church. Worship was good, but again I was overwhelmed with the loss of my husband and the normal birthday celebration we would be enjoying together and tears flowed.

My husband was an awesome man. As I said in an earlier chapter, he had given me fresh flowers every Friday for eight years running. If he failed to get them on Friday from the flower shop, they have been known to call and see if he was all right. His faithful display of love for me was such a witness to that flower shop. They said when they started their Friday special he was one of the first ones to come on board and the only one who had remained faithful week after week.

When Jerry first started bringing me flowers, I can't say I even really enjoyed them. I wasn't really a flower person. They come in fresh and beautiful, and before the week is out, they have wilted and have to be thrown away. He began giving them to me week after week. After a few weeks I said, "Jerry, we can't afford you buying me flowers every week. Would you please stop?" My idea of buying flowers was $15 to $20.00 a pop. Sadness came to his face when he replied, "Sharolyn, they are only $1.50 a bunch and I want to do it because I love you." Talk about feeling like a heel. I was seeing dollar signs and he was seeing another way to express his love and do it inexpensively. From that point on, I loved getting fresh flowers every Friday.

Over the years we collected different vases and Jerry became very good at arranging the fresh flowers of the week in whatever vase he chose. Since it was the weekly special, we never knew what kind they would be, but if there was a choice of color he would always get the deep reds. Occasionally three red roses would be the special of the week. In that case he would buy more than one bunch, as he knew that was my favorite flower.

We moved from our home in town to a home in the country four years into his weekly trip to the flower shop. Even though the move made it a special trip six miles out of his way the last four years, he continued to give me fresh flowers every Friday. Friday came after the funeral and there were no flowers. Again the pain hit me... he was gone. I decided it was my turn to get the flowers. Every Friday I went to the same flower shop and bought the same bunch of flowers that Jerry would have purchased, only now, I was traveling to the cemetery to put them on his grave.

I was standing in the Wednesday night service missing Jerry terribly when one of the pastors of the church began to sing "Amazing Grace." I was standing there weeping unable to sing because that was the song I sang at the graveside service for Jerry. As the song resounded through the auditorium, a woman came from behind me and tapped me on the shoulder. When I turned around, she held in her hand a dozen red roses minus one. God told her to pick them up for me that day. She had no way of knowing it was Jerry's birthday. And the timing could not have been better than with "Amazing Grace" setting the atmosphere in my heart. Minus one was because there was someone at work who was having a "down day" and needed a pick me up. She said, "I hope you don't mind that I gave one of your flowers to my co-worker." Mind! I didn't mind! I was amazed, elated, and touched beyond words.

You never know what God will do. He surprised me with a little "I love you" of fresh flowers that He knew I missed so very much from my Jerry. The big things God does for us are awesome, but it is the little things that show how intimate the Father wants to be with us that amazes me. Only a God as big as God Almighty can be so intimately involved with us as His individual children, to know and do the little things that mean so much to us. Oh how much He loves us!

Chapter 11

Sex? Precious Memories

When Connie and I became widows, we were instantly thrown from married to single. We began having "offers" within three months of being single. We found ourselves in a brand new pool labeled "available" yet our emotions were not saying available. We didn't want a new man. We knew it was impossible, but we just wanted our husbands back. Sometimes the surviving spouse wants to get in a hurry to replace what has been lost. If we act out of loneliness instead of the will of God, we will do things that we will later regret. There are times God does bring that new love immediately, but there are other instances where we have to learn to be content in the state in which we are in by His grace. We decided to address this issue in our book because as young widows, it is definitely an issue.

Connie and I have both lost siblings, parents, and close friends, but those losses do not compare to losing the man with whom you have become one flesh. I mentioned in a previous chapter how my heart ached for Connie over not being able to feel Lee's arms around her again. Now I ached for myself. My bed was empty. My soul mate was gone.

Jerry and I told each other regularly what an honor and a privilege it was to be the other's spouse. Ours was a very intimate, loving relationship. His arms were so strong and his heart so true. I longed to feel the passion of his kiss and his warm embrace, but he was gone. All I had left of that day was precious memories of a life once shared. That part of me had to die with my husband. I cried out, "Father, I am not dead yet! You are going to have to help me!"

It takes the grace of God to walk through the "valley of the shadow of death." Connie and I found ourselves in that "shadow." Jerry and Lee were dead, but we were still walking through a living death. All we had experienced with wonderful, passionate husbands was no longer ours to enjoy. When our husbands died, it was not just a simple separation of two people. It was the tearing apart of one flesh. We had become so interwoven with our husbands in every facet of living that the tentacles of their love reached to the very core of our beings. Chunks of who we were, were jaggedly ripped away, leaving gaping holes.

The synergy of who we were together was gone. Jerry believed in me. He believed in my calling. He supported me and covered me. That is so important and necessary for a woman in ministry. He stood by my side, shadowing me, lending me his strength. Lee was Connie's anchor and her whole world spun around him. They were both men of integrity and honor. Sometimes, you really don't understand the depths of what you have until you lose it.

Someone was found to replace Jerry and Lee in all their previous functions of society. Another manager replaced Lee at the Hutchinson Wal-Mart store. Other men filled Jerry's duties at his job. Another man filled the character Jerry played in our Easter production. But who our men were to our children and us cannot be replaced. What you *do* can be replaced, but who you *are* can never be replaced.

It is not hard to submit to a man who gives his life for his wife and family even as Christ gave Himself for the church. Sure we had our tiffs, but making up was fun to do. Both of our husbands gave themselves to their families. They were lovers, and their quiet waters ran deep.

Connie and I have talked many times how we could understand people turning to alcohol, drugs, or illicit affairs to console their sorrows and loneliness. We both knew that was not the answer, and that wasn't the life we wanted for our families or ourselves. Alcohol, drugs, or sex only compound the problem. The love of God is the only real answer.

Everything comes to us with a thought, and that thought

is a seed. If the seed is allowed to continue in our thinking it will produce after its kind. Thoughts were coming to our minds as to how we could escape the pain and satisfy the unfulfilled physical desires. We would not be telling the truth if we said we had never had the thought to drink excessively or indulge our physical desires. The enemy tempts us all at our lowest point with whatever he hopes we will accept and fall prey to, but by God's grace we don't have to allow the thought to continue in our thinking. It is much easier to get rid of a seed than it is a crop.

Close to a year after our men died, we began joking about finding a man for the night. Of course, not just one man, we needed two. At first, the joking was funny to us, but the tempter was coming with a "seed." It wasn't long, the Holy Spirit spoke very strongly in our hearts. "If you keep feeding the enemy's thought into your spirits, one day you will act on it. Is that the kind of life you want?" No! That was not the kind of life we wanted for our children or ourselves. What Connie and I thought to be an insignificant joke between us, the Holy Spirit labeled as a seed/thought from the enemy. Our physical desires had to surrender to the will of the Father.

Connie and I, by God's grace, have been able to be deeply transparent with each other all through our covenant relationship. Being able to talk out our weaknesses and pray together before each other and God, with gut-level honesty and transparency, has kept us accountable. Every one of us needs that person in our life with whom we can be transparent so the enemy can't get a hook in us. When we have been able to get our emotions and the things we were struggling with out in the open, God in His grace and His mercy has cleansed it away. He set it up that way. "Confess your faults one to another so you may be healed." James 5:16

Faith is our personal surrender to the will of God in every season of our lives. Does it hurt the flesh to surrender to God's will? Sometimes yes! The flesh wants what it wants. Much of the time we use our faith to give our flesh what it wants. When you stop to think about it, it's amazing how much of our prayer time is used to believe God for comfort, luxury, and more enjoyment to our physical life. God wants our physical life to prosper and be in health, but He also wants us to use our faith to walk uprightly before Him regardless of our circumstances, or how much it kills our physical desires to do so.

Whether it was the will of God or not for our husbands to be taken from us so young is a fruitless debate, but widowhood is the state we are in. What is not debatable in our hearts is keeping sexually pure before God. I Thessalonians 4:7, 8 (Amp.) states, "God has not called us to impurity, but to consecrate ourselves to the most thorough purity. Therefore, whoever disregards purity, disregards not man, but God whose very Spirit He gave to us is holy, chaste, and pure." To even think in terms of disregarding or ignoring God is a fearful thought.

We have cried out over and over, "Grace, Father, Grace! Help us walk surrendered to Your will at this time in our lives. Keep us pure and holy before You." Faith is a daily, moment-by-moment, surrender to His will. Faith is leaning everything we are, the entirety of our personality, on Him. When we begin to think we are innocent and strong enough in ourselves to stay pure and holy, look out! Statistics say there is a moral looseness in the "church" today. It is only by His grace, surrendering to His will, we are kept pure and holy. It is not by our works, or our ability, but we have learned, as with anything else, we have to guard our hearts.

We have watched what started to be a good movie, and have had to turn it off. It wouldn't even have to be a sex scene. All it would have to show was a passionate kiss, and we could be sent down a mental trail, stirring up desire for what was no longer ours to enjoy in this season of our lives. It is a dangerous thing to play with thoughts of desire. If we do not reconcile ourselves to the fact that sex outside of marriage is sin, we will compromise. Song of Solomon 3:5 says, "I charge you O daughters of Jerusalem ... do not stir up or awaken love until it pleases (God)." When God brings that new love into our lives then those passions can be reawakened in the marriage bed.

God has promised to be our husband and He is so faithful. He has not left us void of intimacy, but in our worship to Him, He has filled us with Himself. He has surrounded us with His presence, and brought us into spiritual intimacy with Him. We were created for intimacy with the Father. With Song of Solomon we have prayed, "Kiss me with the kisses of Your mouth." If this sounds crazy to you, you just haven't experienced it. You haven't had to push past the physical and find peace to your sexual desires from the only husband we have now, our Father God. Even so, now and then the natural man rises up saying, "What about me?" This is a continual walk of surrender by the grace of God.

So, at this time in our lives what is sex? "Precious memories, how they linger, how they ever flood our souls. In the stillness of the midnight, precious sacred scenes unfold."

Chapter 12

I Don't Know. Let Me Ask Your...

The boys would come to me asking to do something or buy something after their dad died, and the response I would catch myself giving them was, "I don't know. Let's ask your . . ." Life goes on and questions don't stop, and they certainly don't get easier with teenage years. I continue to pray, "Oh God, give me wisdom. You've promised to be the Husband to the widow and the Father to the fatherless. Please don't let me mess up motherhood." I still go to their Father, but it is now their *heavenly* Father. He has proved to be so faithful to guide me and alert me when guidance was needed.

One night the boys had a sleep over and an "R" rated movie was smuggled into the house. I could not sleep that night, so I began to pray as to why I couldn't sleep. About 1:00 A.M. I felt so strongly I should get up, go upstairs, and check on the boys. The movie was playing, and my sudden presence in the room caused embarrassment. Reprimands followed, the movie was taken, the TV turned off, and the party was over.

The next morning my son came into my room thanking me for coming up when I did. The movie had turned ugly as I was coming up the stairs, but he said he didn't have the "guts" to turn it off. Peer pressure is so strong. My children were discovering the Holy Spirit wasn't going to let them get away with much, and I was learning to listen to the Holy Spirit more closely. I was also learning He wasn't going to allow me to get away with much either.

The main bathroom needed redecorating, so it became one of my many projects. The flooring changed from carpet to ceramic tile, and new ceramic decanters were purchased to dress up the vanity. One morning, a decanter was accidentally knocked off the vanity, crashed to the floor and shattered. I came unglued and exploded on my son, accusing him of not caring whether anything was nice or not, and that he didn't appreciate all my hard work, and on, and on, and on as only an angry mother can do. I stormed out of the room leaving him in the stinking hot air I had left behind. I didn't get very far before the Holy Spirit began reprimanding me. It went something like this. My son had not sinned by accidentally breaking the decanter, but I certainly had by my reaction to his accident. What was I getting all huffy about anyway? The decanter was only $3.99. The simple suggestion in my heart was, "Buy two if it's that important to you!" Then I had the choice of being proud and declaring, "I'm

I Don't Know. Let me Ask Your...

99

the parent here," or walking back to my son, humbling myself, and apologizing for my reaction to his accident. I chose to apologize. I could not stand being out of fellowship with my son, and the Holy Spirit. God was definitely working on my character. Character matures by the decisions we make.

One of the hardest decisions I had to make was a legal matter. Since Jerry was killed in a car wreck, there is an insurance settlement still pending. My law firm discussed with me the benefits of including a clause in the insurance claim against my son who was driving the car at the time of the accident. If any fault of the accident was placed on Brian, we could then receive the balance of the claim from our own insurance company. This is done all the time, and it sounded good to be assured of getting full retribution regardless of the court's decision. Rationalism says it's just insurance companies' feuding as to how much each one is going to pay anyway. I felt a check in my spirit and had to pray and discuss it with my kids before I would give an answer.

I sat the kids down and asked them what they thought about me including Brian's name as a clause in the settlement. Of course, I assured Brian again that we did not believe there would be any blame placed on him, but if there were, how would he feel about being named. He assured me that it would be okay and wouldn't bother him, but in my spirit I had this feeling I have to go ask your Father. As I prayed after the kids went to bed that night, the answer became very clear.

God had been teaching me that "covenant-breakers" are the same thing as being "faithless." For me to put my name against my son would stand in the archives of time that I had broken covenant with my son and our family covenant would have been broken. When I saw that financial gain was taking my focus away from family covenant, and I was actually considering breaking covenant with my children over money, it made me angry.

I think Christians are beginning to wake up to the fact that we have chased prosperity, finding ourselves with a whole lot of things, but the covenants of our households are falling apart. Covenant relationships have to be valued higher than anything else in our lives. The seed we sow today doesn't just affect us. When we break covenant with those whom God has put us in relationship, we are opening the doors in the heavenlies for covenant breaking to be a part of our children's heritage. Jesus asked the question, would he find faith when he comes. It takes faith to continue in covenant with another person, particularly when something or someone appears to be more appealing.

I am so grateful for the check of the Holy Spirit that would not let me give an answer that day. When I saw what the real issue was, there was no deliberation at all. I had my answer. The next night I called the kids together again, and told them I would not bring my name against my child's for any amount of money. I was in covenant with them, and I would not break covenant with them for any reason. In the Spirit, you could feel a yoke come off of the family, and a new peace settle into our home. We had moved up another level as a family, even as had happened to us on our trip to California. The battle is won or lost in the spirit, not in the natural. No matter what happens in the settlement, by God's grace we will walk in covenant. God has not left us fatherless.

Chapter 13

Presents or Presence

The first year after Jerry's death, after the kids would leave for school, I would find myself from time to time in a heap on the floor, sobbing. Many times all I could say was the same thing I had prayed prior to Lee's service, "I worship you. I worship you. You are sovereign." The emotional and physical pain was so great it would literally take my breath away. "This is the air I breathe, your very word spoken in me" began to gurgle out of my spirit. There wasn't any dynamic faith-filled confessions flowing out of me, or power shouts. The only confession I had was with much weeping and weakness, "I am dependent upon You, Father, for my strength, my very life, and the air I breathe."

Words are inadequate to express our weakness, our tears, and our groanings. The only time we could find strength was in worship to our Father. When we came into His presence, we could find the solace and the comfort, the refuge and the strength we needed. The worship services at church would take Connie and I into the Father's presence, and tears would flow. We didn't care what people thought of our tears.

Most of us don't know how to handle brokenness, our own or others. We don't like brokenness because we think of it as weakness, and faithful people aren't supposed to be weak. We are to stand on the word unmovable and unshakable. Unanswered prayer isn't supposed to happen, if you have enough faith. If you don't get your answer, you didn't believe enough, you didn't confess enough, or maybe you sinned, and opened a door to the enemy. That all may be true, but it also may be true God has a sovereign will and is engineering our circumstances for a purpose of His own. Regardless, if prayers aren't answered according to our expectations, there is brokenness to deal with. Our brokenness was bringing us to an area of surrender where we had never been before. We were learning, in a very real way, surrender to the Father's will in the darkest season of our lives.

~Connie~

I felt so helpless. I was sitting at the bottom of my stairs feeling so lonely. We were having a major family crisis, and Lee wasn't here to help. What do I do? One of our daughters was struggling, and I really didn't know how to handle it. I started blaming God for Lee not being here. I told God, "You know, there is nothing You can't do. Why didn't You give us some kind of warning about Lee's heart so that he would still be alive? We need him!" I called Sharolyn to see what she was up to, but I was so depressed I didn't want to talk. I finally told her I was depressed and was going to hang up. She pleaded with me to talk it out, but I hung up anyway. I don't ever remember a time I was so negative, but I really didn't care that night. I just wanted to go to bed and forget what was happening in our lives.

The next morning, I woke up to Sharolyn on my doorstep. I didn't want to see her, but she was already there. She came in, sat down on the couch, and said, "All right lets have it. What's up?" I didn't want to talk, but I knew she wasn't going anywhere until I did. I told her how I was feeling and demanded to know why God couldn't have saved our men. All of my pent-up emotions gushed out including, "Why couldn't Lee and I have grown old together? My children never knew a grandfather, and now their children will never know Lee as a grandfather." I saw people in good health in retirement years, and it made me mad that Lee and I could not have had our retirement years together. As I was talking I could feel the resistance against my circumstances in my heart. Why wasn't life turning out the way we had planned it?

Sharolyn started talking to me, and as she did, the Holy Spirit began to speak to me. What I heard was, "Connie, you're not coming against the situation, you're coming against Me, a Holy God. Do I not have the right to be God in your life?" In a moment of time, I saw all the resistance in my heart directed personally against the Most High God. He made me understand that He was in control of all my circumstances, orchestrating them to bring about His purpose for my life. Again I knew it wasn't about me, but about Him and His Glory. I hit my knees and repented begging forgiveness and declaring, "I surrender," over and over.

As I began to surrender my will to His will, all my angry emotions and the resistance to God started to leave. I also noticed other things that had been bothering me didn't matter anymore. His joy and peace came into my heart, and I knew everything would be okay. I didn't know how He would take care of the present crisis we were facing, but God was still God. His grace would be sufficient for everyone. He is so awesome!

~Sharolyn~

The words to a song, "When the music fades and all is stripped away and I simply come, longing just to bring something that's of worth that will bless Your heart," spoke deep within my spirit. My music had faded. In memory of Jerry, I purchased a new keyboard for the worship team, but I had no desire to play it. It seemed there was nothing in me to give into the worship team that had been so much a part of my life for so many years. All I could do many times was let the corporate worship of others wash over me while I cried out for God to hear my heart. This was because no words were coming from my mouth.

The love of my life had been "stripped away." I came to the Father crying out for His presence. I felt like I had nothing left worth anything to bring to Him Things, talents, and abilities held no value to me. My strength was gone. Then the Father began speaking to me, "The only thing you have that has ever been of any value to Me is your heart surrendered to my will. Your surrender to my will, even in the midst of the darkness that surrounds your life, is real faith, and the voice of that surrender is worship."

I remember someone during this time saying they were believing God for a new car. They had picked one out and were claiming it as theirs. Connie and I used to get excited about believing God for things and agreeing with others, but at this time in our lives, things were not important to us. Our houses were full of things. They were all presents from loving husbands, representative of a life that once was. The function of our homes still continued on. The bills continued to be paid. The laundry and the dishes continued to get done. The cars continued to get regular maintenance. There were even a lot of home improvements and new purchases being made. From all outward appearances, our homes were running fine, but what we wanted and needed was Presence to fill the empty, gaping hole in our hearts our husbands left behind.

God began making a comparison in my heart concerning the church and widowhood. The church has all the adornments of a time when the presence of God was real in her midst. The function and activity of the church continues to go on. It still looks like a church and acts like a church, and from all outward appearances the church is running fine. But in some cases, the presence of God is no longer there. Sadly, we don't even know exactly when His *presence* left us. We didn't even realize it had happened, as we are so focused on His *presents*.

I've had much time to think since Jerry's death, and now I question when he actually went home. You see, medically we can keep the body functioning for quite awhile through artificial means without any brainwave activity. To my knowledge, an EEG was not done on my husband. Was there brain activity, or did his spirit actually leave us at the time of the accident instead of five days later?

We can ask these same questions of the church. Is God's presence still in our midst? Is He still producing the brainwave activity for the body to function, or are we pumping up the body through artificial means, keeping programs that have long since died functioning? Where God's presence is, there is power to produce. Man has quite a bit of power to produce on his own. Sometimes we mistake our own ability and talent for God's producing presence.

As long as Jerry and Lee were here, we didn't give a lot of concentrated thought to their presence. Their presence was that constant, steady, factor that gave sustenance to our living. We knew we would grow old together. Our drive was for newer, better, bigger, and more of whatever. Suddenly, our paradigm was changed. Without Lee and Jerry's presence, we felt uncovered and exposed. We became desperate for the Father's presence. We had to have His love surrounding us.

Connie and I began gulping chunks of the Word, reading whole books of the Bible, many books a day, or reading one book of the Bible over and over in our private times with the Lord. We would "camp" on whatever gave us life and share with each other what God was speaking to us. We began seeing the Word through a brand new paradigm. Everything we thought we knew, and the confidence we had in our faith and our abilities was gone. We felt like we had been taken to ground zero. Everything in us was humbled. We were dependent on God's grace for everything. We were at the lowest we had ever been, and if God didn't lift us up, we had no strength to do it ourselves. We began to do as the scriptures said in Psalms 27:8. "Seek My face. Inquire for and require My presence as your vital need. My heart says to You, Your face, Your presence Lord, will I seek, inquire for and require of necessity and on the authority of Your Word."

I began to repent of all the times I had not required Him as the vital necessity of my life. I was busy with church work. Sometimes we can get so busy with doing "good works" we fail to keep our priorities in the proper perspective. God began to speak to me about what it meant to require Him as the foremost necessity of my life.

For someone with kidney failure, the foremost necessity of their life is to be diligent with dialysis on the days and times designated. Their life depends on them keeping that schedule. A friend may call asking them to go shopping at the designated treatment time. There is no choice between living and shopping to be made when your life depends on having that treatment.

I had made choices between spiritual living and shopping or projects. After all, I could take care of my personal relationship with God later, at a more convenient time, when there wasn't something else pressing. The problem with that is the enemy will see to it that there is always something else to distract you from your personal time with God. Your personal time with God can become so hit and miss, it certainly could not be accused of being the foremost necessity of your life. As I read chunks of the word, requiring Him as the foremost necessity of my life, I began to see a side of faith I had never seen before.

Our paradigm of faith was centered on our ability to receive from God. We were products of thirty years of comfort teaching. By this, we mean having faith only for health and prosperity. We believed God for everything we wanted or needed, and all of it had to do with our comfort in one way or another. We believed God for the houses we are now living in. We continue to believe God for our healing when we are sick, and we believe God to bring in finances. God has been so faithful and has given us so much comfort all through the years, blessing us over and over. This is certainly a side of faith tried, tested, and proved, but there is more to faith than this. Faith is our personal surrender and worship to God regardless of our circumstances. Several years ago I was given an example of personal surrender.

When I was nine months pregnant with our son, Brian, Jerry and I were plumbing a bathroom in the new addition to our house. We were in the crawl space running the four-inch drain line into the main sewer line. Going under the house, I just barely fit through the access hole. The drain line was a straight shot directly beneath the access hole, which narrowed the opening even more. While we were doing the plumbing, we didn't realize we were impeding the path to get out.

I tried to get out of the access hole, but I wouldn't fit. Jerry was ready to cut the pipes. All he could see was having a baby in the crawl space. This was Saturday and Brian came the following Monday. It occurred to me if I would stop trying to get myself out which caused me to bulk up even more, causing more resistance, I might still fit. Jerry got out of the crawl space and took my hands stretched upward to him. He began to pull so slowly I thought he would never get me out. The slower he pulled I wondered if he had the strength to pull me out, since being full term I was so heavy. Since I could not help myself, I was dead weight, but what was in me was new life. I was totally dependent upon him being strong enough to pull us through. He was pulling slowly because he didn't want to hurt the life of our unborn child or me. I had to trust him leaning all of me into his grip.

That is how surrendered God wants us to be to Him. In the hard places of our lives where we find ourselves so heavy laden with any number of things, God says, "Lift your hands to me. Surrender to My strength and My will. I can pull you through." When He pulls us through, we are a witness to His love and grace in the midst of good or bad. Only in surrendering ourselves to the grace of God can our dead weight be turned into brand new life.

Faith is rejoicing in the midst of troubles and sufferings, knowing that life's pressure and affliction and hardships produce patient and unswerving endurance. Another way of saying this is it produces the fruit of the Spirit. The Spirit of God is the very character of God or who God is. Acts 1:8 says that we are to be filled with the Spirit of God or the character of God so we will be witnesses unto Him. Being filled with the Spirit is allowing the fruit of the Spirit to be developed in our lives until we produce the evidence of that fruit.

The fruit of the Spirit is revealed only when we come to the end of our own fruit. When we are put in the press of life we will witness to something. I will never forget when I heard in my spirit, "Sharolyn, your anger does not promote my righteousness." The fruit of the Spirit will not be witnessed in our lives as long as we are claiming our right to our self. The fruit of the Spirit is only displayed as we surrender our life to the Father not being concerned with self-realization. This was certainly a new understanding from my theology that faith was all about me and my wants and my desires.

Our personal surrender in worship to the love of the Sovereign God will carry us through the hardest of circumstances. It will bring peace in the midst of the storm. One of the first things we want to do in the midst of a storm is lose our peace, which is a fruit of the Spirit. In the absence of peace, the enemy has freedom to plague us with panic, anger, and fear, none of which promote the righteousness of Christ. Panic comes in the midst of a crisis. Anger comes in the midst of an assault. Fear comes in the midst of a bad report. Sometimes all three come at once. Hebrews 10:12– 13 says, "Christ, after He had offered a single sacrifice for our sins sat down at the right hand of God to wait until His enemies should be made a stool beneath His feet." If we will surrender to the Father and allow the fruit of the Spirit of peace to rule in our hearts by the grace of God, the enemy cannot stand against us.

Peace is also the shoes necessary as part of the armor of God. Keep your shoes on. Don't kick off the shoes of peace in the midst of a storm. The enemy will become a footstool for Christ as we learn to keep him under our shoes of peace. When Jesus comes, He is looking for people without spot or blemish and at peace in serene confidence, free from fears and agitating passions and moral conflicts. (II Peter 3:14) He is waiting for us to develop into His likeness, His image, and His character, walking in peace with our faith based on the love of God regardless of our circumstances.

It is easy to become "favorite word" people. We enjoy certain passages of scriptures that promise us comfort. That is like eating our favorite dessert, but there are other scriptures that depict the development of our character that sometimes take us through hard places for the glory of the Lord to be revealed. That is the liver and beets of the scriptures. Not many people want to endure liver and beets. One day the Lord spoke to me that the body of Christ was anemic in character. We tend to believe our foot firmly planted in the word of comfort should be able to skirt us around the circumstances God could be engineering in our lives to mature us into a "perfect man thoroughly furnished unto every good work." We don't want to spend much time in scriptures declaring we may have to go through hard places to gain.

If our faith based in comfort doesn't deliver us to our expected end, some have even said, "This faith stuff doesn't work. I quit!" Quitters do not understand that the experience was not the end in itself, but a gateway into a deeper understanding of the character of God being developed in their lives. Faith surrenders to God in the midst of what appears to be defeat. Surrender will bring us to a higher level of faith and power, working for us a far greater weight of glory. What appears to be defeat has a way of turning into victory if we will endure long enough to see below the surface of the experience to the revelation of the glory of God.

We, as parents raising our children, know there are stages to a child's development. As small children, we totally meet their needs and wants according to their age. As they grow, we begin to give them responsibility and more privileges. We test their level of responsibility and character from time to time. If they fail the test, we, as parents, have been known to unsettle our child's comfort by disciplining them through grounding or taking away items until they mature more in their character or ability to handle the privilege.

I remember when our boys were able to ride their bicycles to their friends' houses, we were adamant about them telling us where they were going. From time to time, we would call and check to see if they were where they said they would be. If they weren't there, we dealt with the trust issue and keeping their word. If we couldn't trust them with a bicycle how would we be able to trust them with a car? Why do we think God our heavenly Father would be any less interested in our character than earthly parents?

The other extreme are the few people in this world who really like liver and beets. There foot is so firmly planted in the message of the sufferings of Christ bringing us into His character and into His glory they never partake of the goodness of the promises. Balanced faith is having one foot firmly based on His promises while the other foot is firmly based on the love of God regardless of what life dishes out to us. Then with the three Hebrew children we can say, "Oh King Neb, whether God delivers us or whether He doesn't we are still not going to bow to you." Basically they were declaring with Paul, "Nothing, death nor life, can separate us from the love of God." If your foot is not planted in the love of God, regardless of your circumstances, as well as His promises, you will bow. God just may be raising the bar of having a love relationship with Him in our lives today.

Chapter 14

Can Things Really Work Together For Good?

When Jerry and Lee died, Connie and I found a roadblock placed on the pathway of our lives. We thought we knew where we were going and how we would get there, but in an instant all that was changed. When there is a roadblock, you have to find another way. Our old life as we knew it was gone, but God immediately began resurrecting us to a new life in Him. There have been many discoveries on this journey in our new life with Him.

One of the most important discoveries was that our faith cannot be based upon our circumstances whether they are good or bad. Our faith has to be based upon the love of God in the midst of our circumstances. For too long we have based our faith on circumstances and we typically have no steadfast, patient endurance. If our faith is only based on the good things that God does for us, and we find ourselves in a season where nothing good seems to be happening, we will question God.

My family hit a pocket of "bad things." In the natural, I am sure it looked like we had no faith and God certainly could not love us. After my husband, Jerry, was killed, my father had a stroke Christmas Eve. Holidays are hard enough after losing a spouse, but when emotions become complicated with yet another devastating hit, the stress compounds. My father had been in the hospital from Christmas to January 31st incapacitated from the stroke. Arrangements had to be made for hospice. I was in the process of signing hospice papers when my cell phone rang. Brian had been in another accident. Brian had been driving on snow and ice when our truck slid off the road and hit a tree.

This time I arrived before the ambulance. Brian again had another concussion and suspected internal injuries. Again, we needed airlifted to Wichita. In the ground ambulance before the emergency helicopter arrived, I laid my hand on Brian, and out of my spirit came the declaration, "Not this time."

There was a supernatural peace and strength that held me as I was alone on the road when they sent me out of the ground ambulance to communicate the extent of the injuries they had assessed on Brian with the helicopter crew. In the darkness amidst flashing emergency lights, I leaned into the ambulance and felt the presence of the love of God surround me. As I drove to Wichita for the second time chasing a helicopter, it seemed like the second verse of the same song less than three months earlier. The difference was the peace I felt in my heart. Brian was released within 24 hours.

Five days later, my father passed away and my brother and I were sitting before yet another mortician. Our mother was so sick with the flu she was unable to get out of bed so she was not able to attend the funeral. We moved her into my home to aid her recuperation. The time she spent with me was a time of healing and restoration for a daughter and now a mother in the midst of widowhood in less than three months.

Within six months my oldest son totaled his car. In my heart I heard, "Trust Me. I am hardening you to difficulties." Such peace came in my heart as my car headed once more to the aid of yet another son. All of these things happened in less than a year following Lee and Jerry's death. In the midst of each event that happened to us, out of our spirits came the words, "I worship," the voice of surrender. It wasn't anything we did, but by His grace those words would come, and His grace would bring us peace in the midst of whatever we were dealing with.

The capstone of all these events was receiving the headstone for Jerry's grave on the weekend of what should have been our 23rd wedding anniversary. I had just returned from the cemetery and was sitting on my front porch reflecting on the year's events with my heart full of emotion, when I got a phone call. The reason for the call was to ask, "After all you and your family have been through can you truly say that all things really work out for good?" This is an honest question. Of course they were referring to the scripture in Romans 8:28 that states, "All things work together for good to those who love God, to those who are the called according to His purpose."

Yes, we can truly say all things are working together for our good, but one must read on to the end of the chapter. The rest of the chapter talks about being "molded into His image" and "bringing us into right standing with Him." Paul even asks, "Who shall separate us from the love of God. Shall suffering, affliction, tribulation, calamity, distress, persecution, hunger, destitution, peril, or sword?" That pretty well sums up anything that can happen to us. It certainly doesn't say these things won't happen. Paul says in all these things we are more than conquerors because nothing can separate us from the love of God.

God doesn't look at the outward appearances. He looks to see if the heart is surrendered and if the reflection of His character is there. He is more interested in our relationship with Him and His character being formed in us than in our comfort. Sickness or poverty won't keep us out of the kingdom of God, but loose morals and an unholy character will.

Sorrow, pain, sin, and suffering are all facts of life. We can try to evade these facts through many different means, including using our faith, but at some point we find ourselves having to embrace them. We have mistaken having to embrace pain as a lack of faith, or our faith is not working. That is not the case at all. Suffering will tend to do one of two things depending on our response. It has the power to destroy us or it has the power to remove the shallowness from our lives filling us with deep compassion that can nourish others. Real faith works by love. Faith that has not come through the fire can be harsh and uncaring.

Through all these events, I became progressively empty of myself. Suddenly my words to God were unimportant. All that was important to me was His words to me. Silence came upon my mouth and heart to heart communication began to flow. I would sit for hours or walk in my woods in silence, just listening. At times, His presence would so fill my heart it would feel as if I could hold no more. Again I felt my breath taken away and my eyes flooded with tears, but this time it wasn't from pain. His love was so overwhelming.

He began to give me songs with words, and at other times there would be songs without words. Out of the depths of my spirit would come a melodious sound that all I could do was lend my vocal chords for its utterance. The worship was unencumbered with inadequate words. Pure worship was wafting up to the Father from the very depths of me and then again my breath would leave as He overwhelmed me with His love. One morning I was listening to the birds and their song was so sweet. Each species was harmonizing with all the others. "How beautiful!" escaped my lips and instantly I heard the Father say, "Your voice is sweet to Me!" and His overwhelming presence caught me again.

Many times Connie and I have felt as though the Father was slipping up behind us when we would least expect Him wrapping us in His arms of love, enveloping us in His presence like our husbands used to do when we were busy in the kitchen. There isn't any announcement or fanfare. It is just a spontaneous show of affection in the stillness of the moment and again we are captured by His love.

If we would only take the time to know the depths of God's love and feel the warmth of His embrace. Perhaps you've heard the saying, "Love is better felt than telt", meaning the love of God is better experienced than talked about. We can in a moment give him our list of requests. Our job jar is ever ready with our "honey-do list" of what we want. We get so caught up in things and works that we ignore relationship. Relationship takes time and time is of the essence since we have so much to do.

God isn't interested in what we can accomplish for Him. One word spoken through us birthed from the lips of Almighty God can accomplish more than a lifetime of our works. He is interested in our intimate relationship with Him. Without intimacy in the natural there will be no birthing of children. Likewise, if we never experience intimacy with the Father there will be no birthing in the spiritual. We will continue to be stuck in our dead works going round and round the same issues. Oh how much the Father wants a love affair with us! How much He desires to draw us into His presence and progressively saturate us with His love, birthing new life through us.

God is looking for a people that are interested in knowing what He wants, taking on His characteristics, allowing the fruit of His spirit to be witnessed from their lives. Our focus was changing. It wasn't about what we wanted from God anymore. It became about what He wanted from us. What we have discovered he wants from us is becoming invaluable to us. He wants our word. He wants our integrity. And, He wants our faith, our personal surrender to Him- but so does the enemy.

Chapter 15

Our Walk of Surrender

All through our lives we will have difficult experiences with which to deal, experiences that will test our word, or our integrity, or our faith. There is a war going on in the heavenlies and it is over those three issues for each one of us. We are learning to make our decisions based on the issue that is at stake in the heavenlies rather than what we see it to be in the natural. Things aren't always as they appear. Sometimes, what we think to be a simple, insignificant decision is a seed sown in the heavenlies speaking very loudly for or against our earthly life. If you want to tear down principalities in your life begin making your decisions based on the issue at stake in the heavenlies.

We will be tested over whether we will keep our word. It can be something as little as taking your child for ice cream to "I will till death do us part." It is not a real test if it is not an appealing alternative to what we have committed to. The decision is to watch over our word to perform it no matter what new information may be introduced. New information will be enticing and try to cause us to change our mind. Then the value of what or whom we have committed to becomes insignificant in our eyes. It was such a small thing. They will understand if we don't follow through with what we are committed to. "They" may understand but our word and our trustworthiness have been compromised and it has been noticed in the heavenlies. He who is faithful in the little things will be faithful in the bigger things. Unfaithful seed produces a harvest of more unfaithfulness and allows the enemy the advantage in our lives to eventually destroy our covenant relationships. It all starts with a seed.

Remember the story I gave in an earlier chapter regarding an insurance settlement against my child for more financial gain. Breaking our word or breaking covenant with those in whom we are in relationship with can be disguised in many different forms. We have to hone our skills of looking below the surface appearance. What is really the root issue of this difficult place in which I am finding myself?

Maybe God has given us a word or a promise that is His covenant to us, but it has taken too long for it to come to pass, as with Abraham and his son Isaac. When the word or the promise we have been given becomes our objective rather than *God* being our objective, we will produce an Ishmael. We still have "Holy Wars" today. The promise is just the exercise of our faith. Our personal surrender to God is the objective of our faith.

Our integrity will be challenged. Will we be honest no matter the cost to ourselves, or will we withhold information because we think it is to our advantage? Abraham's integrity check was telling Sarah to say she was his sister. That wasn't totally a lie, but that also meant it wasn't totally the truth. Abraham's fear for his life caused him to fail the integrity test. Many times we want the promise or the gift without the level of character required to maintain, and keep it. Fear will cost us our integrity and a lack of integrity will cost us our promise. We may have already received a promise, but if we make decisions out of fear of personal cost, compromising integrity, we will lose the promise.

My family continues to be in the midst of settlement over Jerry's death. The issue of dispute has been over whether our car had one headlight or two. We signed sworn affidavits that our car had two headlights. Our entire family believed we had two headlights at the time of the accident. Brian and his father had gone through the car together from front to back prior to putting it back on the road; however, the other driver continued to say we only had one headlight.

I began to search for someone who could verify that we had two headlights. I just knew I would find someone to witness to that fact. Instead, one of our good friends saw us pull away from their house a few days prior to the accident after dark with only one headlight. I was devastated! Now a portion of the fault of the accident was mine. Immediately a little voice in my head said, "You don't have to tell anyone what you found out." I began to rationalize that we had told the truth so far as we knew it in the original affidavit, so we weren't lying. I'm just not telling all I know. If I presented to my attorneys what I had found out, it certainly would not help my case. That would not be good. Fear of losing surfaced. How many times we have teetered in that grey zone of not really a lie but not really the truth and chosen what looked best to our natural mind. My integrity was being challenged.

I presented what I had discovered to my attorneys, and they passed it on to the opposing side a day or two before our scheduled depositions. When my son was questioned concerning the headlight issue, without hesitation he answered with the new information. The opposing attorney stopped the deposition and looked at me. He began to tell us - in the attorney business - how refreshing it was to find honest people. He asked if I had asked anyone else about the lights after I had found out from these people we only had one. I told him to ask further was pointless. I believed the word of our friends.

Questions, questions, and more questions proceeded, but the opposing attorney was so kind in all of his questions to my family. He asked if any of my children had turned to alcohol or drugs since their father's death. "No, we were all learning dependence upon God's grace. God had been good to us, and we were learning to be a family pulling together, not apart. We have actually became closer as a family." God was giving us peace in the midst of the questions, and I could feel the presence of the Lord in the room. The court reporter and my attorney's eyes welled with tears. Events truly do give us the opportunity to be a witness.

The second day of depositions, I met the driver of the other vehicle involved in the accident. There was such a peace in my heart and gratefulness for everything he did at the scene to help my family after the accident occurred that I was able to shake his hand and thank him for his help. There was no anger toward him for the death of my husband. Then, after all the questions, I thanked the opposing attorney for his kindness in questioning my family. He explained that as an attorney he saw a lot of people who deserve to be beat up in this world, but our family didn't deserve that. With moist eyes he confided that he knew what my boys were going through because he had lost his father when he was 18.

The case is still unsettled but what is settled is the peace that is in our hearts. There is no greater joy than to know the peace of God in your heart and in your household after having walked in integrity by the grace of God. Our decisions make the difference, not only for us, but also for our future generations. When you surrender your way to the Father and trust Him for the outcome, you move the hand of God to work in your behalf in the heavenlies.

I can tell you for sure, having walked through two days of depositions with three attorneys, a court reporter, an investigative officer, and the other driver in the sufficiency of God's grace makes everything else I have to deal with seem like small potatoes. I have truly experienced the love of my Father and He is more than able to keep everything I surrender to Him, but that is something you have to prove for yourself.

Finally, our faith will be tested. How surrendered are we to God when our comfort is unsettled by unsettling circumstances? Are we shaken when disagreeable events happen in our lives, or are we so surrendered to the Father that we will stand regardless of the circumstances? Are we more devoted to the presence of God, or the promises of God? Abraham was tested on that point by being asked to sacrifice the promised son, Isaac, to the Presence of a Holy God. He was being asked by that act, "Who do you love more, Me or the promise?" Abraham passed the test and became all God promised. He now knew his Father so well having walked with Him through such diverse and difficult circumstances his choice was to surrender to God.

There is a war going on in the heavenlies and the war is over our word, our integrity, and our faith. When you are in the midst of difficult and challenging circumstances don't have a knee-jerk reaction, but look to see what issue is being challenged in the heavenlies. Every decision we make influences the heavenlies to our advantage or to our disadvantage giving either God or the enemy leverage in our homes. This is how we tear down principalities.

To be forewarned is to be forearmed. Connie and I are praying that the words of this book will bring understanding to those of you who are in the midst of the strain of crushing difficulties. The trials we endure on our journey of life are not ends in themselves, but they are gateways through which we become more intimately acquainted with the love of God reflecting more of His character.

Consider it wholly joyful whenever you are enveloped in or encounter trials of any sort or fall into various temptations. Be assured and understand that the trial and proving of your faith brings out endurance and steadfastness and patience. But let endurance and steadfastness and patience have full play and do a thorough work, so that you may be people perfectly and fully developed with no defects, lacking in nothing.

-James 1:2-4

Thank God we are growing up in character. God is raising the bar of our relationship with Him. Seek His presence in the midst of the storm. You won't be disappointed.

Our walk of faith, or better said our walk of surrender, is a journey into the very heart of God. It is by a continual walk in the grace of God, through our personal surrender to the Father, that we are being saved. It is not by our works, our gifts, our talents, our abilities, or even our ability to believe God for "things" that we receive salvation. So, we really can't boast. The only thing that has ever been worth anything to the Father is the total surrender of ourselves to Him.

It is not a one time surrender. We must surrender to Him in every season of our lives. Connie is currently facing the issue of living alone. Her youngest daughter will be getting married in a few weeks. She will again have to discover the sufficiency of God's grace in another new day in her life. I am continuing to trust the Father to give me the wisdom to raise three boys to be men of integrity and honor like their father. I have found myself saying from time to time, "I don't know how to raise three boys." God spoke in my heart after I said it the last time that He didn't want to hear that anymore. It's by God's grace that we are able to know how to do anything and His mercy is new every morning. We must continually "Trust in the Lord with all our heart, and lean not to our own understanding (trying to figure things out), but in all our ways (every issue, event, or circumstance of our life), acknowledge Him (surrender to Him), and He shall direct our path (our journey into His very heart). Proverbs 3:5-6 That is the faith that will take us all the way Home.

Epilogue

The Journey Continues

At the time of this writing it has been nearly two years since our husbands' deaths. It seems as though we have lived one life and now we are living another. Our first life is gone but we have been left with a multitude of wonderful memories. Connie and I have just returned from a trip where the four of us used to go together. We sat in the waiting area to be seated at one of our favorite restaurants seeing again in our mind's eye the fun we had there in days gone by. Embracing reminiscing in places once enjoyed seems to bring comfort and more healing. We are also discovering that creating new memories in new places brings healing and helps to create the new life we are now living.

God is so faithful to begin to bring a new resurrected life out of the dust of the old life if we will allow Him to. New life comes by increments. Life is a process that has a way of bringing new joys to hold and new life to embrace.

Connie's son David and his wife Sandy are expecting their first child in December of 2003. Connie is soon to be a grandmother! Such excitement fills her heart when she visualizes what it will be like to hold the little guy for the first time. She has a month long trip planned to get all the time she can with her new grand baby.

David and Sandy are both in management positions at Wal-Mart. David is currently a co-manager waiting for his own store and Sandy is an assistant manager. As you can see David is following in his father's footsteps.

Kellie and Nick Moore live in Hutchinson, Kansas. Kellie, like her father, is also in management as an assistant manager for a national food chain. Nick is currently finishing his bachelor's degree in history. They will be moving away from Hutchinson in a year for Nick to obtain his doctorate in history. His goal is to be a history professor.

Stacy is in the midst of wedding plans. Jason Brown proposed to Stacy March 2003. The wedding date is in August. There is still much to do to get ready but she is so organized and detail minded that it will run smoothly. Stacy is an orthodontics technician. She is head technician and again finds herself in management and oversight. Jason never knew Lee but he knows him because his memory lives on. Jason is a Correctional Officer. Jason and Stacy plan to stay in Hutchinson for a year after marriage and then move to Missouri to further their education.

As I am writing this I am reminded again of the prayer Jerry and I prayed the day we buried Lee that his mantle would pass on to his family. I believe it has in a very real sense. What a wonderful heritage they have.

Nathan Sidebottom is currently finishing his associate's degree at Hutchinson Community College with his sites set on WSU to study anthropology. He continues to work for Wal-Mart while he finishes his education. The fence we built is still up and the goats are corralled nicely in the pasture. Hallelujah!

Brian will be a junior in high school the fall of 2003. Mechanics is his delight. He will be pursuing classes as he finishes his high school education to achieve his goal as quickly as he can. He loves music. He plays rhythm, lead, and bass guitar, as well as drums.

Jonathan will be in eighth grade this fall. Video games are his delight. He has grown so much this year he is almost passing his older brothers in height. That will be a sad day for the older brothers but Jon says "It rocks!"

The Beginning...

This is a new beginning in a new life with a new fragrance for Sharolyn and Connie. They know what it is like to have been in a river of grief that tried to overtake them, but the river, and the water, and the currents are changing, and the joy of the Lord is being released in their lives. There is a new ship arising that they are putting their hands to. The wind is changing and they are going in a new direction. The river is carrying them gently to the new port that God has for them by His design and His purpose.

Connie and Sharolyn just spoke for Newton, Kansas' St. Luke's Presbyterian Women's Meeting the end of April. They will be speaking at the Women's Aglow in Lakeland, Florida in mid-July, as well as at an Independent church in Wichita, Kansas later that same month. St. Luke's Presbyterian Church has already requested their return in September to speak at both of their Sunday morning services.

Requests are coming in for them to share their story of friendship and the amazing grace of God in the midst of extreme pain and heartache. Clearly, there are many who struggle with having the courage to face the ordinary events of life after tragedy strikes. The two friends are filling a schedule that will take them to many places in the coming months to proclaim that:

> *"Nothing can separate us from the love of God*
> *as we are held in the grip of His grace."*

Authors' Contact Information

For information/bookings, etc.
please contact Sharolyn or Connie at:

Walk With Me Ministries, Inc.
PO BOX 456
Hutchison, Kansas 67504-0456
or
contact Family Solutions, Inc. at
(888) 361-9473
(405) 376-4401(fax)